Durham City Remembered

Durham City Remembered

Michael Richardson

breedon **books**
PUBLISHING

First published in Great Britain in 2002 by
The Breedon Books Publishing Company Limited
Breedon House, 3 The Parker Centre,
Derby, DE21 4SZ.

To

L.R. II

Most of the photographs can be ordered by writing to:

The Photographic Archive
Beamish
The North of England Open Air Museum
County Durham
DH9 0RG

ISBN 1 85983 291 1

Printed and bound by Butler & Tanner, Frome, Somerset, England.

Cover printing by Lawrence-Allen Colour Printers, Weston-super-
Mare, Somerset.

Contents

1935 8

1936 14

1937 29

1938 41

1939 54

1940 63

1941 67

1942 72

1946 73

1947 78

1948 88

1949 98

1950 104

1951 114

1952 121

1953 131

1954 144

1955 153

1956 165

1957 173

1958 184

1959 199

1960 207

Foreword

I FEEL very privileged to be asked by Michael Richardson to write the Foreword for his latest work *Durham City Remembered*, because his books are the finest illustrated record of the history of Durham.

I have lived in Durham almost all my life and I feel a great sentimentality when I see all the old photographs of our city. Virtually every photograph in Michael's book reminds me of my youth and brings back so many fond memories.

The period up to the 1960s was when I was in my teens and was a time which saw the beginning of so many changes to Durham. The face of our city began to alter considerably. So many photographs depict scenes that have now disappeared, scenes which many people reading this book will have forgotten about and will be delighted to recall. There is nothing like looking at old photographs and reminiscing about them. Each photograph has a different poignant memory for each person.

Michael's books – this is his ninth – are an outstanding contribution to the history of Durham. Most history books tend to be 'dry' and difficult to read unless one has a real interest in the subject (I speak with a certain amount of authority, having once been a history teacher) but Michael's books are certainly an exception to this. They become a riveting read once they are picked up and immediately become a topic of conversation with whoever is present when you are reading them. The reader constantly asks questions: "Look at this…"; "Can you remember that?"; "I can remember when…" This latest book is no exception.

No more from me. Start reading this book and you will have hours of enjoyment. If you have lived in Durham all your life, then you will almost certainly see someone you know in its pages. If you did not live in Durham during these times you will be enthralled by what the city was like all those years ago.

Gerry Steinberg MP
City of Durham
2002

This book is supported by
Nelson's Removals of Durham; The Arts and Humanities Research Board; North East England History Institute; Archibald's Builders Merchants; Miss H.C. Webster; Local Artist; and Beamish Museum.

If any readers have new material (*ie* photographs, slides or negatives) on Durham City and the surrounding area, or any information, the author would be pleased to hear from them. Telephone: 0191 3841427.

'Preserving and Presenting the Past for the Future'
The Gilesgate Archive

Introduction

This collection of over 500 photographs has been brought together in one volume to cover a specific period of life, in and around Durham City, from 1935 to 1960. This is the first time that such a comprehensive collection has been put together. (There are no Gala photographs shown as they have been published in a separate volume, *Memory Lane: Durham Miners' Gala 1935-1960.*)

The book is laid out in chronological order beginning with a fine portrait of Durham's oldest Freeman, Mr John Vest, aged 90, of Pity Me. There are numerous sporting photographs throughout, which show the strong link Durham people have had with competitive sports. The student 'Rag', once one of the highlights in the Durham calendar, is well-covered. The Silver Link Bridge, linking Gilesgate to Pelaw Wood, is seen on the day of its opening, 12 April 1938. As we get to 1939 many of the photographs show preparations under way, for the beginning of World War Two – gas mask drills, Land Army training at Houghall and air raid precautions exercises.

It is noticeable that the Durham Ice Rink has played an important role in the leisure life of Durham people. Because of World War Two, there was a shortage of photographs due the limited supply of film (If any reader has photographs from this period, I would very much like to hear from them). After the war, in October 1947, Mr Tilly is photographed showing German prisoners-of-war around Durham Cathedral. The same POW's returned to the cathedral in December that year to present gifts of toys to be placed under the Christmas tree.

In May 2002, the Queen, as part of her Golden Jubilee celebrations, visited Durham City. Her first visit to the city was in October 1947 (see p.87).

This year marks the 50th anniversary of the 1st Battalion Durham Light Infantry's departure for Korea. It is seen marching into the city for a special farewell service in the cathedral.

If you have had connections with the city between 1935 to 1960, you will almost certainly recognise familiar faces here. If you have had no connections, then this volume will help to explain why Durham City is such a special place.

New material still turns up in the most unlikely places. Recently an original framed photograph showing the opening of the first public library in Durham City was found in a skip. Permission was received to retrieve it, and it now has a safe home in the Gilesgate Archive. What will turn up next is anyone's guess. However this is a good time for me to stop, and for you to look at the photographic treasures this volume contains.

Michael Richardson
2002

Acknowledgements

So many people have donated and loaned photographs to the Gilesgate Archive, that it is impossible to thank them all individually. Special thanks go to: Mr J. Armstrong, Mr F. Bilton, Mr J. Birch, Mr J. Battong, Mrs P. Black, Mrs J. Blair, Mrs V. Brown, Mr W. Carr, Mr B. Cole, Major R.S. Cross, Mr E. Dobson, Mr I. Forsyth, Mr G. Gilson, Mr R. Gleason, Mr G. Hales, Mr J. Harrop, Mr W. Helm, Mrs M. Howdon, Mr R. Hopps, Mr P. Jefferies, Mr J. Lawson, Mr C. Lloyd, Mrs Lye, the late Mr I.M. McIntyre, Mrs M.J. McIntyre, Mr G. Marley, Miss D.M. Meade, Mr T. Middlemass, Mr Mollon, Mr G.R.S. Nelson, Mr A. Nichols, Mrs A. Nicholls, Mr R. Norris, Mr and Mrs B. Pallis, Mr D. Patterson, Miss Reed, Mrs N.Richardson, Mr A. Rippon, Mr Ian Robinson, Mr T. Rowntree, Mr G. Steinberg MP, Mrs M. Shotton, Mr M. Summers, Mrs J. Taylor, Mr R. Thompson, Mr I. Walker, Dr C.D. Watkinson, Mr K. Williams and Mr D. Young.

The staff of the following institutions have helped in various ways: Durham University Library, the Dean and Chapter Library, Durham Clayport Library, Durham Record Office, *Northern Echo*, *Durham County Advertiser*, *Sunderland Echo*, The Photo Shop, Carrville, Breedon Books, The History of Durham Project and St Edmund's Women's Fellowship; Bearpark.

1935

Durham's oldest Freeman, Mr John Vest, on his 90th birthday, photographed on 3 January 1935. He lived at Pity Me and his good health enabled him to visit Durham City every week.

The man with the 'coldest job' in the city, a stonemason working on scaffolding at the topmost walls of Durham Castle, January 1935. Note the wooden poles fastened together with rope.

Mrs Susan Kingston, centre, a grand old lady of 83, enjoying teatime treats given by Bearpark WI at the Colliery Institute for the over 65s, 8 January 1935. She was the mother of Alderman W. Kingston of Bearpark. After tea entertainment was provided by pupils of Miss Lillian Ainsley's dancing school of Durham. Men were given an ounce of tobacco and ladies half a pound of tea.

The new building belonging to Mackay's carpet factory, April 1935. The cottages on the right were later demolished to make room for the ice-rink. The green area is the Durham County Girls' School (now the Sixth Form Centre) playing field.

Alexander's Jewellers, 1 North Road, April 1935. In 1902 Mr M. Alexander began business in South Shields and later went on to open several branches in the north. The Durham branch opened in May 1926. The site is now occupied by the Halifax Building Society. The poster on the right is advertising the Palace Cinema in Walkergate.

One of Matthew Fowler's removal wagons from New Elvet, seen at Crossgate Peth, April 1935. This business, including that of Auctioneer and Estate Agent, was established in March 1906, when a small office in Durham Market Place was rented at the premises of Messrs Swanson. He later took over part of the property of Joseph Johnson's Brewery, New Elvet. The railings on the right protect the slope of Crossgate Peth.

A group of schoolboys from Sherburn Village visiting the printing works of the *Durham County Advertiser*, 45 Saddler Street, June 1935.

The opening of Durham County Hospital bazaar in Durham Indoor Market. Amongst the guests on the platform are Lady Surtees, Dean Alington, Lady Londonderry and the Bishop of Jarrow, Dr J.G. Gordon, 22 October 1935.

'We will remember them', a picture taken on Remembrance Day at Brancepeth Village smithy, showing the horseshoe archway. The blacksmith, Robert Tindale, had succeeded his father in the business, 11 November 1935. The young boy is his son, Geoffrey.

The Bridge Hotel, North Road, near to total destruction after the fire which occurred shortly after 3.30am in the bar, 27 December 1935. The fire was so intense that nearby homes had to be evacuated; fortunately no one was injured. The landlord was Mr Alexander Burr. The fire was attended by the City Brigade and the Houghton-Le-Spring Collieries Fire & Rescue Brigade.

An interior view of Earl brothers' confectioners' shop, 68 Saddler Street, October 1935. People queued for their famous meat pies. The shop was next to Masons the Chemist (now Waterstone's).

The Roman Catholic Gala procession leaving Palace Green with the Children of Mary, 1 August 1935. High Mass had been sung earlier in the day in the picturesque grounds of Springwell Hall, North End, which later became St Leonard's Roman Catholic School.

1936

Red setter puppies, six out of a family of 13 belonging to Mr & Mrs Frederick C. Goodyear of Lowes Barn, Elvet Moor, January 1936. Fred was the son of Alderman Frank W. Goodyear, builder and brickyard owner.

Craftsmen of Durham are seen in the ancient workshops of Durham Cathedral, January 1936. They are Walter Hollis (centre), W.S. Cope (right), and young Thomas Jopling (left), who is standing beside the magnificently-carved door which was dedicated 29 January to the memory of his grandfather, the late W.H. Jopling. The carving of this door, which is the north entrances to St Cuthbert's Shrine was begun by Mr Jopling shortly before his death and was completed by Mr Hollis.

Soldiers from the 8th Battalion Durham Light Infantry, in procession to the cathedral for King George V's memorial service, 28 January 1936. The Dean, Dr C.A. Alington, gave the address to a congregation of about 4,000.

The Northern Counties' Amateur Brass Band Association contest at Durham drew bands from all parts of the county, 1 February 1936. Lumley Colliery band won two trophies. The picture shows an interested crowd listening to one of the bands.

Councillor J. C. Fowler, Deputy Mayor of Durham, presenting medals & bars at the annual social gathering of St Margaret's Church Lad's Brigade, 25 February 1936. On the right is Major H. Cecil Ferens.

A crew from St Mary's College landing at Brown's Boathouse after rowing the course 26 May 1936. They had been taking part in a timed race with Armstrong College, Newcastle. The Armstrong crew won by 19 seconds.

Durham Colleges 'Rag' students, 17 June 1936. They were about to tour the surrounding districts selling the 'Rag' magazine in aid of the Durham County Hospitals. Three days later, the airship Hindenberg passed over the city.

A performance of *The Wraggle-Taggle Gypsies* by Durham Folk Dance Group at Brancepeth Castle's Folk Dancing Festival, June 1936.

Students from St Hild's College, photographed tidying the cathedral churchyard, with young helpers, during the Mothers' Union Festival, 13 July 1936.

An assembly of mothers outside the north door of the cathedral after the Mothers' Union festival service. The Revd Canon O.C. Quick preached the sermon, 13 July 1936.

'Telfer's Boys' Harmonica Band, Framwellgate Moor, July 1936.

A group of excited boys from East Howle School, Ferryhill, playing on the gun in the courtyard of Durham Castle, 11 August 1936. The gun was a trophy from World War One.

A works outing from Holiday's brick works, Sidegate, 19 September 1936. Thomas Holiday, the owner, is pictured on the extreme right, photographed in Durham Market Place prior to departure.

The City Fish & Game Co., 3 New Elvet, October 1936, showing Mr S. Hedley, the fishmonger, arranging the open window display.

Durham Civic Plate, and that of the old Trade Guilds, displayed in the Town Hall, when members of the National Association of Cathedral Old Choristers were visiting Durham, 19 September 1936. Eighty representatives from 16 associations took part.

The wedding of Miss Elizabeth Alington and Lord Dunglas, MP, Durham Cathedral, 3 October 1936. The daughter of Dean Alington, the bride wore a gold-coloured dress. After the ceremony 500 guests attended a reception at the Deanery.

A group of the Jarrow Marchers stop for dinner near Farewell Hall on their way to London, 9 October 1936. About 200 men had set off from Jarrow to hand in a petition against the level of unemployment and also the means-test. While here two medical students from London attended to their blistered feet. Charles Errington, an ex-Northumberland Fusilier cook prepared a tasty pan of broth for the marchers' lunch.

Mr G. Cummings, gardener for the Dean & Chapter, the occupant of Nursery Cottage, Quarry Heads Lane, Durham, photographed after gales of 70 miles per hour hit Durham, 27 October 1936.

Lady Londonderry, Mayoress of Durham, drawing aside the Union Jack at the formal opening, revealing the name, 'Alington Place', 11 November 1936. These 24 houses, named after Dean Alington, had been erected at Mill Lane, Gilesgate, by the Church Army Housing. They were built for low-wage earners with large families; rents were 7s 1d for a 3-bedroom and 7s 4d for a 4-bedroom.

The Bishop of Durham (Dr Hensley Henson) dedicating Alington Place. Left to right, the Revd C.K. Pattison, Revd G.H. Aird, vicar of St Giles's Church, and the Bishop with Lady Londonderry, 11 November 1936. Mr D. McIntyre designed the houses, which were built by Councillor, F.W. Goodyear. The Dean and Chapter contributed £200 towards the cost.

A house party at Wynyard Hall given by Lord and Lady Londonderry, the new Mayor & Mayoress of Durham, November 1936. Left to right, standing: Lord Londonderry, Herr von Ribbentrop, the German Ambassador, Sir Ronald Graham, Mrs Roger Lumley, Mrs Kerr, Mr Roger Lumley, MP for York, Lord Durham, Sir Hedworth Williamson and Lord Castlereagh. Seated: Lady Durham, Frau von Ribbentrop, Lady Londonderry and Lady Castlereagh.

Herr von Ribbentrop and Lord Londonderry, November 1936. von Ribbentrop had been the guest of Lord Londonderry and was later to attend a civic service at Durham Cathedral on the 15th of that month. At the end of the service the British and German National Anthems were played by the cathedral organist, Mr Conrad Eden.

Belmont schoolboy's football team, 1936. Back row: J. Lisgo, J. Clough, Mr Spavin, E. Passmore, J. Mallion, Mr Venner, B. Sutherland and J. Nixon. Middle row: Jos Davies, Bill Garside, E. Dobson, L. Tempest and Jack Coulson. Front row: W. Scott and Reg Martin.

City of Durham Football Club, c.1936. (formed c.1919). It won the North Eastern League Championship 1924-25, and was runner-up (DivisionTwo) for the season 1930-31. Among the internationals produced by this club were G. Camsell, S. Crooks and G. Stevenson. Back row, left to right: F. Footer (chairman), G. King, R. Woolrych (trainer), J. Harrison, N. Swales (captain), J. Blenkinsop, G. Moore and F. Woolrych (secretary). Front row: J. Burns, S. Glidden, R. Littledyke, W. Towers and H. Emery. Sammy Crooks went on to play for Derby County and England. George Camsell made his name with Middlesbrough and England.

Durham St Nicholas FC, *c.*1936. Member of the Ryhope and District Wednesday League, this club was formed in 1929. In the season 1934-35 it reached the final of the City of Durham Medal Competition and in 1935-36 was in the final of the League Challenge Cup. Left to right, back row: G. Grabham (secretary), B. Humphreys (committee), R. Sands, W. Scarr, W. Atkinson, J. Routh, R. Roxborough (captain), G. Scarr and G. Gales (trainer). Front row: G. Dimambro, W. Craig, G. Porter, N. Fleming and R. Peele.

Belmont Red Triangle FC, *c.*1936, member of the Durham City and District League. In the season 1932-33 it won the Sherburn Aged Miners' Homes Cup and reached the final of the Durham City and District League. Back row, left to right: T. Miller (committee), J. Lee (committee), T. Rowntree (committee), H. Byfield (trainer), H. Robson (committee), H. Barker, J. Laws, T. Bunce, J. Bell, J. Palmer, E. Makepeace (chairman), W. Marley (secretary) and R. Marley (committee). Second row: C. Riley (captain), H. Wilson and T. Cooper. Seated on the ground: T. Unsworth, W. Coffey, T. Sommerbell, C. Thompson and J. Hamilton.

Sacriston Football Club, *c.*1936. Twice winners of Chester-le-Street Ambulance Cup and Durham Hospital County Cup, also Durham Central League Champions on two occasions. Back row, left to right, back row: J. Embleton, J. Smailes, F. Anson, M. Mordue, N. Crossman, J. Chapman (captain) and C. Shields. Front row: G. White, T. Darwen, R. Drape and O. McGinn.

Bowburn Welfare FC, *c.*1936, member of the Durham and City District League. It won the Durham Aged Miners' Cup and Durham District Knockout Cup in 1933-34 and 1935-36; also the Sherburn Aged Miners' Cup 1933-34. Back row, left to right: G. Arkwright (committee), J. Fishburn (secretary), W. Atkinson, W. Burbanks (committee), L. Roberts, P. Lovatt, S. Bestford, C. Mitchell (committee), J. Flannagan, S. Mould (committee), S. Heatherington, R. Arkwright (committee) and R. Freeman (committee). Front row: H. Burnett, R. Spence (captain), A. Allison, W. Mitchell, H. Alderson and J. Tipland (trainer).

West Rainton Labour Party FC, *c*.1936. Back row, left to right: I. Bowater (committee), W. Kelly (committee), R. Groswaite (trainer), M. McIllwraith (committee), R. Vine (committee), J. Vine, E. Bates, T. Teal (committee), W. Dawson, G. Dunning (vice-chairman), W. Fawcett, J. Sheldon (chairman), J. Lawrence, E. Dunning (committee), J. Storey (committee) and E. Griffiths (committee). Front row: G. Perry (secretary), F. Hall, R. Wise, J. Willis (captain), S. Wheatley, W. Perry and T. Kelly.

Brandon (Social) FC, *c*.1936. Member of the Durham Central League, it was formed in 1931. Its best season was 1934-35 when it won the League, Deerness Aged Miners' Cup & Brandon Nursing Cup. Back row, left to right: D. White (trainer), J. Oliver, A. Birch, A. Clough, W. Dixon, W. Ruddock (captain), and T. Dodds. Front row: J. Joyce, D. Breen, R. Halliday, E. Carter and H. Pickney.

1937

The unveiling of the portrait of Dr J.S.G. Pemberton, President of the Council of Durham Colleges, at Durham Castle, 16 February 1937. Left to right: Mr T.C. Dugdale, (the artist), Dr Pemberton, the Marquis of Londonderry (Chancellor of the University), who unveiled the portrait, and the Bishop of Durham (Dr Hensley Henson).

Some of the 100 members of the Durham County Constabulary on the southbound platform at Durham Railway Station, 11 May 1937. They were drafted to London to assist in street duties on Coronation Day (12 May). On the left is Supt. Knaggs of Chester-le-Street. Note that some are wearing their First World War medals.

Graceful young dancers, who were trained by Misses E. & S. McCoull of the Morton House School of Dancing, Tynemouth, photographed after they had enjoyed a happy night at the Town Hall, 12 April 1937.

Dancing pupils of Miss Smith and Miss Marjorie Liddle assembled in the Town Hall for their annual ball, 24 March 1937. They disported themselves in many of the latest dance movements before a large audience.

A delivery boy making his way back into the city from Pimlico at the top of South Street, March 1937.

Robert Dixon of Belmont, working at Holiday & Co Ltd, Manufacturing Chemist, Claypath, April 1937. He was one of two lucky young lads chosen to represent the Belmont Branch of the YMCA at the coronation of King George VI in London.

Newspaper House, 64 Saddler Street (the office of *The Durham County Advertiser*), decorated for the coronation, received first prize for the best-decorated Durham City business premises, 12 May 1937. The building was originally that of the North Eastern Banking Company, and was built in 1898.

The march past after the coronation service in Durham Cathedral, Sunday, 9 May 1937. Various groups of Church Lads' Brigades, Scouts and Guides from the county took part in the procession, as well as a detachment of the 8th Battalion Durham Light Infantry.

The Mayor of Durham, Lord Londonderry, at the saluting base on Palace Green after the coronation service in the cathedral, 9 May 1937. Others in the picture are Colonel W.B. Greenwell, Lady Londonderry, Mr & Mrs W.R.H. Gray (Deputy Mayor & Mayoress) and Alderman F.W. Goodyear.

A garage fire near 'Bunnygarth' The Grove, North End, Durham City, the residence of Mr John McAlmont, 26 May 1937. The city fire brigade tackled it but the garage and the car were totally destroyed. About 30 rare birds from a nearby aviary had to be released for fear of them being killed by the fumes; only two were re-caught.

The entrance of the heralds prior to the crowning of the May Queen, Joan Francis, aged 10, at Bluecoat School, Claypath, 24 May 1937. This festival was started at the school in 1933.

The Mayor & Mayoresss, Lord and Lady Londonderry, with pupils of Bluecoat School at their Empire Day festival, 24 May 1937. Lady Londonderry was photographed amongst the girls who had formed the choir.

A group photo of Durham City golfers at Mount Oswald with their special guests Alfred H. Padgham and the open champion, Henry Cotton, 27 May 1937. They took part in an exhibition match played over 18 holes; Henry Cotton won. The event was organised as part of the club's Jubilee programmes.

The 'Tipster' at the Durham 'Rag' races, 18 June 1937. The *Durham County Advertiser* carried the humorous caption, 'I've got an 'orse! I've got an 'orse! The owner's going to back it. The trainer's going to back it. I want you to back it. It'll romp home at 33-1'.

Bearpark schoolboys' football team, June 1937, winner of the Deerness Valley Schools' League Shield and the Ushaw Moor Aged Miners' Cup. Back row, left to right: Mr Walter Grainger, Eric Joyce, Robert Seed, Leslie Colwell, Joseph Corker, Thomas Minns, Thomas Wilson and Mr Thomas Wilson. Middle row, seated: Dennis Belshaw, George Ruddick, Ronald Thompson (captain), Mr Herbert Chicken (headmaster), Edwin Winn, Lawrence Smith and Mr Aaron Pearson (deputy headmaster). Front row: James Smallwood and Robert Thornton.

The students' representation of the 'Mayor and Corporation' complete with sword, and mace-bearers and bodyguard, at the 'Rag' procession, Palace Green, 18 June 1937.

University policemen, Sergt-Major Gray, ex-DLI, left, and Sergt. William Plunkett on Palace Green, July 1937. The University police are believed to be older than the county force, having been formed around the time that the first students were admitted in 1833.

The visit of the Duke of Kent to the Haig Homes, Sutherland Place, Sherburn Road Estate, 13 July 1937. The Mayor, Lord Londonderry, is seen to the right wearing his chain of office. The street was named after Sir Arthur Munro Sutherland who had contributed substantially towards the cost of the homes, 18 houses were built with a rent of 6s 7d per week. The Haig Homes movement owned 361 houses and flats in 13 centres throughout the country.

The Duke of Kent being greeted by the headmaster of Durham School, the Revd H.K. Luce, 13 July 1937. The Duke was the first member of the royal family to visit the school. During a conversation with the headmaster the Duke asked that his visit might be commemorated by an extra day's holiday. It was understood that the wish was complied with. The school chapel, a memorial to past pupils who were killed in World War One, stands high on the hill.

A physical fitness display at the city cricket ground on The Racecourse at Durham, July 1937. On the far right is the Pineapple Inn, Old Durham Gardens.

The funeral procession of the Deputy Mayor, Councillor W.R.H. Gray MA, JP, approaching the cathedral, 28 July 1937. He died suddenly on the evening of the Miners' Gala while attending dinner with the miners' leaders at the Royal County Hotel. He was the son of the late Mr William Gray JP and was a former pupil of Bede Model School, Gilesgate. On the death of his father he took over the business of University Robemakers & Gentlemen's Outfitters in Saddler Street and also opened a branch in Newcastle.

The deferred coronation tea for old folk from the city. The venue was Durham Indoor Market, 22 July 1937. The Mayor, Lord Londonderry, presented the oldest man and woman with £1 each.

Giant 'puff balls' monsters of the fungus world, which were growing near Kepier, October 1937. Some have been known to grow to such a size that they have been mistaken for sheep from a distance.

Mayor's Day at Durham, 9 November 1937. Lord and Lady Londonderry are photographed, prior to the swearing in of the new mayor. They are seen with members of the bodyguard and, at the rear, Alderman P.J. Waite. The new mayor was William Ewart Bradley.

Durham school children at the Palladium Cinema, Claypath, December 1937. A special Christmas treat had been organised for them by the *Durham County Advertiser* readers. On the right is Alderman T.W. Holiday, owner of the Palladium, The lady on the right is Minnie Clark, wife of Benny, who had the toyshop opposite.

Excited children at the Palladium, December 1937. The boy second from the left is Ronnie Clark. Around 800 children from poor homes in the city were entertained. Packets containing fruit, sweets and a new penny were presented to each child. The Palladium was opened 18 March 1929.

Milkmaids at Durham County Council's Farm, Houghall, December 1937. The photograph was taken as part of a national campaign to promote the benefits of milk as the nation's cheapest food.

1938

An unusual view from the inside of T. & C. Heslops' butcher's shop, 85 New Elvet, now Prontaprint, February 1938. W.J. Heslop started the business in May 1895 at 4 New Elvet. In about 1937 it became a limited company when Mr R. Morton came in as a partner with the founder's two sons.

Staff outside the United Shoe Shop, Elvet Bridge, *c.*1938, showing Vince Edwards, in the white apron, and, second from the left, Wilf Mollon. The shop was to the left of Bramwell the Jeweller. It later moved to Saddler Street.

Skilbeck's Garage, Langley Moor, March 1938. The firm was established at Annfield Plain in 1913. Councillor R. Bone JP, Chairman of Brandon & Byshottles Urban District Council, officially opened the garage 2 March 1938.

Cheerful children from Bluecoat School, Claypath receive sand-shoes for their sports activities, as part of the government's national fitness campaign, February 1938.

Mrs C. Bowers of Greenfield Terrace, Sacriston, with her dog Jack. She was believed to be the only woman Caller (knocker-upper) in the mining districts of England, February 1938. Every morning at one o'clock she would leave her warm bed to call the miners up to go to work on the fore-shift. She first started the job as a wartime occupation during World War One.

Mr Elijah Burnside, watch and gramophone repairer, of Brandon, who was blind from birth, March 1938. In his spare time he enjoyed entertaining folk with the playing of some of his several musical instruments.

A 'Keep Fit' class of enthusiasts from the Durham City Girls' Club going through their exercises inside the Drill Hall at the bottom of Gilesgate Bank, 19 February 1938. Front left is Annie Shea.

Playtime at St Godric's Roman Catholic School, Castle Chare, March 1938. The street in the background is Co-operative Terrace, which was demolished when the new road was built linking the Millburngate Bridge to North Road roundabout.

An unusual view of the window-cleaner, showing off some of his acrobatic skill at the *Durham County Advertiser* office, 64 Saddler Street, March 1938.

The opening of the Silver Link footbridge, which connects Gilesgate with Pelaw Wood, 12 April 1938. Alderman J.T.E. Dickenson, on the left, opened the bridge in the presence of the Mayor, Councillor W.E. Bradley. It was designed by the City Engineer, Mr J.W. Green, based on a larger one which crossed the Victoria Falls on the Zambezi River. The Cleveland Bridge Company of Darlington constructed it. A model of it is still on permanent display in Durham Town Hall.

Durham Cathedral Choir, April 1938, photographed in the chancel with the Neville Screen and the Rose Window in the background.

President of the Hospital, Lord Londonderry, laying the foundation stone for the £60.000 extension to the Durham County Hospital, North Road, 7 May 1938. He had just recovered from a fractured collar-bone, suffered during a golfing holiday with the Prime Minister in Scotland.

Mr H.S. Harrison, Chairman of the Durham County Hospital Management Committee, explained the necessity for the extensions of the work at the hospital, 7 May 1938. The firm of Cordingley & McIntyre designed the extension and the builders were George Gradon & Son, North Road.

The newly-opened Neville Dene Hotel (now The Pot & Glass), Crossgate Moor, 7 May 1938. It was opened by the Mayor, Councillor W.E. Bradley, and was built by Thomas Clements & Sons Ltd. of Newcastle. The name of the hotel was chosen through a competition, although it is now renamed after the old Pot & Glass which stood at the bottom of Tollhouse Road.

The Student 'Rag', June 1938. The City Corporation, like many other businesses, loaned its wagons and drivers for the annual charity event.

The retaining wall for the footpath near South Street Mill, being built by the Dean & Chapter and Durham City Council, June 1938. On the far left is the spire of St Nicholas's Church in the Market Place.

The funeral of the Bishop of Jarrow, Dr James Geoffrey Gordon, August 1938. The body had lain overnight in the Chapel of the Nine Altars, He was buried near to the South African War Memorial in the cathedral churchyard. He had been appointed in 1932.

Girls from Mackay's Carpet Factory, Walkergate, brushing and finishing off carpets, October 1938. The old factory site is now part of Millennium Place, Claypath.

Rebecca Birch, Herbalist, 25 Market Place, a member of the National Association of Medical Herbalists, October 1938. Health foods were almost unknown in the Durham district before she began business. She served her apprenticeship with her father, John Birch, who had been a qualified Medical Herbalist for 54 years. She passed the final Examination of the College of Botanical Medicine in 1932.

Bower Bank, the name of the lane and area behind St Giles's Church, Gilesgate, October 1938. This name, which is now almost forgotten, is mentioned in St Giles's tithe records in 1655.

Doggart's shop in the Market Place (now Boots Chemists), October 1938. The Durham City shop was opened in 1923. The firm had started with one shop in Bishop Auckland in 1895. By the 1930s it had grown to be one of the most progressive in the north of England.

Gloria Dawn as Cinders, aged 16, December 1938. A pupil of the Durham County Girls' School. Her real name was Gloria Turnbull and she lived in Albert Street, Durham City. She was photographed prior to her debut at a theatre in Darlington.

Mrs Hodgson, her daughter, Eliza and son, John, of New Brancepeth, had a remarkable escape when their car was caught by a skidding omnibus at the entrance to Cross Street (now part of Hawthorn Terrace), next to the Colpitts public house, 19 December 1938.

1939

The King and Queen arrived by the Royal train at Durham Railway Station, where Lord and Lady Londonderry, Lord Lieutenant of the County, received them, 23 February 1939. The main purpose of the visit was to enable Their Majesties to see and inspect the houses that had been erected in recent years on the Sherburn Road Estate.

A royal visit to Durham by King George VI and Queen Elizabeth, 23 February 1939. About 3,000 school-children assembled in the Market Place to sing the national anthem, under the conductorship of Mr Oliver May of Durham Cathedral Choir.

The King and Queen visiting houses on the new council estate on Sherburn Road, 23 February 1939. They are seen leaving the home of Mr and Mrs William Wright of 24 Cuthbert Avenue. Both the King and Queen showed keen interest and Her Majesty was particularly impressed with the internal arrangements. The new Pelaw View Community Centre now occupies the site.

The royal couple are seen prior to visiting the home of Mr and Mrs Thomas Albrighton, 22 Fir Avenue, 23 February 1939. The new estate housed about 3,600 people who were formerly resident in dismal and dilapidated property in the heart of the city, Millburngate and Framwellgate.

The Bishop of Hexham & Newcastle, Monsignor J.M. McCormack, photographed after the blessing of the new Roman Catholic Church Hall (now St Joseph's School, Mill Lane) at Gilesgate Moor April 1939.

The Mayor, Councillor Wilf Edge, and Father W.I. Meagher, with members of the Roman Catholic community outside St Joseph's new church hall, April 1939.

Some of the burnt-out cars that were destroyed at the newly-built garage of J. McIntyre & Son, New Elvet, May 1939. The damage was estimated at £3.000. McIntyre's Coachworks were founded in 1896 at Elvet Waterside.

A lorry belonging to S. Snowdon Ltd with its load of fish which had crashed into a telegraph pole near Farewell Hall on the Great North Road, May 1939. What looks like scratches on the photograph are in fact wires from the nearby telegraph pole, which was hit.

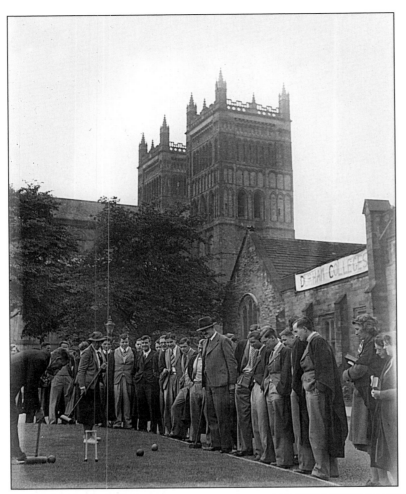

A croquet tournament on Palace Green to raise funds for the student 'Rag'. Canon E.F. Braley of Bede College is seen making a shot watched by Mr J.F. Duff, Warden of Durham Colleges, June 1939.

Students in fancy dress for the 'Rag', one of whom is impersonating Adolf Hitler, June 1939. Three months later war was declared on Germany.

Blind couple, Mr J.W. Vest of Hatfield View, New Elvet, and Miss Annie Morrison of Burnhope photographed after they were married at the Registry Office in Claypath, 10 August 1939.

Children from St Leonard's Roman Catholic School, North End, receiving instructions from Mr G.B. Philipson in the fitting of gas masks, August 1939.

Land Army girls seen feeding pigs during their training at the School of Agriculture, Houghall, September 1939. The girls were there for a four-week course to learn the practical & theoretical sides of farming, so as to qualify for membership in the Women's Land Army.

An Observer Corps crew from the city, September 1939. Names on the reverse are: G. Trotter, J.W. Lambert, T.S. Ritson, C. Maude, M. Mellon, F. Dodds, J.R. Gilderoy, T.H. Mole, N. Carpenter and D.E. Webster.

Training at Belmont Park Racecourse, October 1939. A private company had been formed to promote race meetings at Belmont. The site was chosen because the track had been partly laid already. The area is now part of Cheveley Park housing estate.

Harvest Festival at St Nicholas's Church, Market Place, 8 October 1939. The Revd F.H. Pickering is seen on the right conducting the service.

The Rainton Handicap winner, Belle Toi crosses the line at Belmont Park Racecourse, 6 November 1939.

A procession of men and women who were manning the ARP posts around the city attending a cathedral service, accompanied by the new Mayor, Councillor S. Kipling, 12 November 1939. Preparations for the setting up of Air Raid Precautions posts were started at Durham in June 1938.

An Air Raid Precautions Wardens' exercise, December 1939. Wardens are seen treating 'casualties' in the northern part of the city. The mock casualties were volunteers from the 5th Durham Scouts.

Durham City Observer Corps Headquarters, December 1939. Observer Captain E.G. Jones, MBE, MA, the controller of No.30 group is seen in the background. The man holding the telephone is Mr Donald Webster, Vice Principal of Bede College.

Soldiers from the 8th Battalion Durham Light Infantry outside Gilesgate Goods Station, c.1939. The building, Durham's first passenger station, opened in June 1844. In more recent times it was Archibald's DIY store and has recently been converted into a hotel.

1940

Durham's new ice-rink, April 1940. Miss Iris Howles from Manchester who was 3rd in the British pairs championship in 1937 and 1938. She is photographed with Mr Adolf Schima of Manchester (right) a bronze, silver and gold medallist, and Mr 'Icey' Smith, owner of the rink. Mr Schima had been appointed as a coach at the rink, lessons being 4s for 40 minutes. (Note the open top.)

The 'Dee Cee' Works (toffee factory) of Adams (Durham) Ltd., New Elvet, seen during the fire which almost destroyed the site. Durham City Fire brigade brought the fire under control after a 3-hour effort, 3 April 1940.

A group of ladies assembled in the Prior's Hall of Durham Deanery, working on behalf of the Central Hospitals Supply Service Committee, June 1940. The Hon. Mrs Alington (organiser) is on the extreme left.

Durham Girl Guides and members of girls' clubs who had successfully collected aluminium for the war effort, July 1940. They are seen near Fleming & Neil, ironmongers, Claypath. The old Police Box can be seen in the distance. Dorothy Colman, photographed third from the left, has an extra piece of material added to lengthen her uniform. This was due to the shortage of cloth.

A practice fire call at Durham which was issued by Supt. J.R. Ellwood (in uniform) brought a quick response from his team, photographed near The Sands, August 1940. The building in the background belongs to the sewage works on the opposite side of the river.

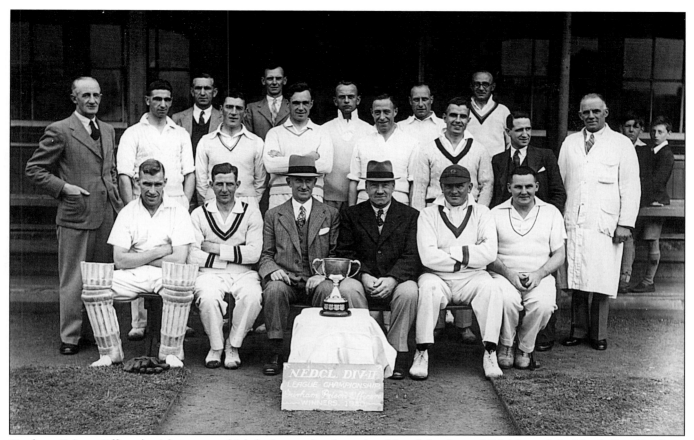

Durham Prison Officers' cricket team which had won the championship of the Second Division of the North East Durham Cricket League, August 1940. Out of 18 matches played, 17 were won and one was drawn. In the centre of the picture is Governor W. Foster and on his left is Chief Officer C. Desbrow.

The Mayor, Councillor Kipling, receiving £6 10s from Vera Tomlinson, Florence Hudson, Elizabeth Chapman and Doreen Chicken, October 1940. This was money they had raised for the Ambulance Fund.

'Bringing in the Sheaves': a member of the Land Army gathering the harvest at Houghall Demonstration Farm, August 1940. The girls were working under the direction of Mr J. Wilson of Houghall Farm.

A window display in North Road organised by the Durham County Allotment Holders' Association, encouraging the citizens of Durham in the 'Dig for Victory' Campaign, October 1940. Mr C. Edmundson of Crook is seen on the right; on the left is Mr L. Buss from Houghall School of Agriculture. People were encouraged to grow onions as, prior to the outbreak of war, most of our onions were imported.

Boys and girls from Bluecoat School, Claypath, photographed after the presentation of junior First Aid certificates, December 1940. Mr H.L. Holliday (right) trained the children and the success rate was 100%.

Jean Reed skating at Durham Ice Rink, *c.*1940. Note the open top.

1941

Five Durham girls, Marion Richardson, Marjorie Summerbell, Ann Crofton, Margaret Hall and Maureen Garbutt are seen presenting a cheque for £3 10s to the Mayor Councillor J.F.J. Smith in aid of the Spitfire Fund, Durham Ice Rink, January 1941. The money had been raised by a concert and collection.

The army salvage unit photographed at a munitions dump near Durham, January 1941. Unexploded German bombs, which had been emptied, were cut up for scrap by the oxy-acetylene flame and then sent to the steel furnaces to make bombs and returned back to Germany.

Rabbi Steinberg congratulating the bride and groom at the Jewish Synagogue, Laburnum Avenue, Durham City, 12 February 1941. The groom, Harold Steinberg, on the right, was the son of Mr and Mrs D. Steinberg of Gateshead, and the bride was Mrs Etta Robinson, the youngest daughter of Mrs and the late Mr M. Robinson of 38 Hawthorn Terrace, Durham City (parents of Gerry Steinberg MP). On the left are Mr and Mrs J. Garbutt (sister and brother-in-law of the bride) who themselves had been married 18 years previously in the same synagogue. The bride's niece on the far right is Miss Cynthia Garbutt, the bridesmaid. Rabbi A.C. Steinberg, brother of the bridegroom, came from Manchester to officiate at the ceremony.

Alderman William Smith, chairman of the City Education Committee, lends a hand in the serving of hot school meals at Bluecoat School, Claypath, 18 February 1941. The occasion was the opening of the city's first school canteen which was under the supervision of Miss D. Holliday, domestic science teacher. The menu consisted of vegetable soup followed by jam roll and custard.

Members of Bearpark Women's Institute, present a pageant 'The Masque of the Empire', 18 February 1941. It was produced by Miss A. Grainger, with all proceeds going to the Durham County Hospital.

Miss Cecilia College, 'Queen of the Ice', centre right, Britain's World Champion Amateur Figure Skater, at Durham Ice Rink, 19 March 1941. She is surrounded by her admirers, among whom is the Mayor, Councillor J.F.J. Smith. She had travelled from her home in the West End of London to take part in the first anniversary ice carnival.

The Deputy Mayor, Councillor S. Kipling, among a group of Boy Scouts in the 5th Durham's den under Durham Indoor Market, April 1941. The occasion was the presentation of 25 junior St John's Ambulance badges and certificates following tests.

Voluntary Services, representing the County of Durham, parade to evensong at Durham Cathedral, 15 June 1941. Many of the Nursing Division and Ambulance Men and Women were from the colliery areas.

Sherburn Hill Auxiliary Fire Service (AFS) photographed on the occasion of the presentation of badges and certificates, 19 July 1941. This event took place in the Seven Stars Inn, Sherburn Hill.

Durham's new streamlined fire engine on display for the first time in Durham Market Place, 27 August 1941. On the left are Councillor Wilf Edge and the Deputy Mayor, Councillor S. Kipling, and Mr J. Willis, the chief officer who designed the engine. The fireman second from the right is Mr H. Young.

An Assistance Board Mobile Unit (for the purpose of alleviating distress arising from enemy action) was shown to the citizens for the first time, 11 October 1941. The Mayor, Councillor J.F.J. Smith, welcomed Mr R. D. Brightman, area officer of the unit.

1942

Members of the Air Training Corps (ATC), during 'Warship Week', 1 February 1942. It was hoped that the target of £210.000 would be raised for the city and rural districts to be able to qualify for the 'adoption' of HMS *Witherington D76*, which was on escort duty in the North Atlantic.

Members of the Auxiliary Territorial Service (ATS), later replaced by the Women's Royal Army Corps (WRAC.), marching over Elvet Bridge when they were taking part in 'Warship Week', 1 February 1942. The parade had started in Waddington Street and travelled through the Market Place where Lord Londonderry, Lord Lieutenant of the County, took the salute. It finally ended in Old Elvet.

Two mobile canteens, which were handed over to the North Regional Fire Service by the British Legion of the County of Durham, 30 May 1942. They had been purchased by voluntary subscription from men and women of the Legion. Mr J.J. Lawson MP received them on behalf of Sir Arthur Lambert, Regional Commissioner, to be used by the National Fire Service No.1 Northern Region. The Mayor was Councillor H.L. Gradon.

1946

The Mayor, Councillor J.L. Robson, and other dignitaries, watching the Victory Parade, outside Shire Hall, Old Elvet, 8 June 1946. Captain R.W. Annand, VC, DL is at the rear of the group.

The City Corporation gave a party to 500 old people as part of the Victory Celebrations, 27 June 1946. The Mayor, Councillor J.L. Robson, seen on the right, welcomed them all. Tea was followed by an entertainment in the Town Hall.

A party of 30 Chinese seamen from the crew of SS *Goldmouth* came to see the cathedral and ancient city, 19 July 1946. The Revd J.R. Kay, Minister of the Congregational Church at Durham, and the Revd J. Patton, Regional Chaplain of the British Sailors' Society, North Shields, escorted them.

The Workers' Educational Association students based at Hatfield College, July 1946. Mr B.W. Abrahart is seen outlining the day's programme while assembled on the steps in the castle courtyard. This was the first school held since before the war. It was organised by Durham University Board of Extra-Mural Studies in connection with the WEA.

Miss Hilda Sides, a distinguished London artist, with some of her watercolours of the city beauty spots, August 1946. Photographed in the ballroom of the Dunelm Hotel, Old Elvet.

Honorary Graduates honoured at Hatfield College Centenary, August 1946. Left to right: Mr John Moor, Henry Smith School, West Hartlepool (DCL); Dr C.E. Whiting former Vice-Principal of St Chad's College (D. Litt); and Dr K.C. Dunham, a member of the Geological Survey, London (DSc), who was knighted in 1972.

A cheerful Matthew Ranson of Front Street, Pity Me, riding his AA patrol motorcycle and sidecar through Pity Me, 8 September 1946. The photograph was taken after his guest appearance on the BBC Radio programme, *Country Magazine.*

Mr W. Tilley, centre, showing German prisoners-of-war round Durham Cathedral, 27 October 1946. They were attending the harvest festival service, which had been arranged by Lieut.Col G.K. Stobart, Officer Commanding the 93rd POW Camp at Harperley. Part of the camp still survives, hidden among fir trees on the road from Crook to Weardale. Some of the men in the photograph were U-boat crew-members.

Mr Jack Winter, an ex-miner, aged 86, October 1946. A resident of the Almshouses, Owengate, looking out of his window towards the spot where he declared he saw a ghostly figure at 1pm on the 12 October. The ghost is said to be that of a University Don who had committed suicide by throwing himself down the black staircase in the castle.

The Princess Royal with Matron Miss Lee, Lord Londonderry and the Mayor Councillor F. Foster, 21 November 1946. The occasion was the opening of the children's ward, Durham County Hospital, which was named after the former Matron, Miss Margaret Whitlock.

Members of Durham Colleges Dramatic Society, wearing 17th-century dress for the period play *Love for Love* by William Congreve, photographed passing through the Watergate at the end of the South Bailey, December 1946.

Corporal Henry H. Wills of 54 Laurel Avenue, Durham, photographed with his mother and daughter, Margaret, outside Buckingham Palace after being presented with the Distinguished Conduct Medal, December 1946. The DCM was awarded for his bravery in Albania, in 1944, while serving with the Royal Corps of Signals; he was later transferred to the Commandos.

Boys and girls admiring the toys which German prisoners-of-war had made to be presented to the cathedral for needy Durham children, December 1946. Note the diamond patches on the prisoners' clothing.

Right and next page: The Dean and Mrs Alington among the German prisoners who had brought the welcome gifts to be placed under the Christmas tree, December 1946. The Dean had lost a son in the war, Capt. Patrick Alington of the 6th Grenadier Guards.

1947

The footpath below Pelaw Wood, February 1947. The old ash tree at the end of the railings was where the Durham Regatta races started. The once overgrown pathway to Old Durham Gardens has recently been resurfaced to make it more accessible. The photograph shows Mrs H.M. Webster and her daughter Hilary.

The Durham 'Hello Girls' who were operating the switchboard at the telephone exchange in the General Post Office in Claypath, February 1947. They were then taking about 12,000 calls a day; five men worked the night duty.

The old iron Baths Bridge, February 1947. This was the second bridge and was erected in 1894; it had replaced an earlier wooden bridge of 1855. The present bridge was opened in 1962.

The Galilee Chapel,
Durham Cathedral,
being swept by two of
the cleaners,
February 1947. It
took these ladies a
week to complete the
task of sweeping the
whole cathedral.

Sherburn Road Youth Centre, Junior Football Team, March 1947. Back row, left to right: John Flowers, Dick McCormack, J. Carr, J. Hurst, Jack Sutherland, Jack Birch, Jim Jordan and T. Stenard. Front row: P. Hanley, G. Marley, L. Balmer, E. Kirby and J. Lake. In June that year it played a German POW team and was charged with playing on a Sunday by the Durham FA. This was illegal for registered players, and the team was suspended for two months.

Veteran runners burning up the track at the Easter Races on The Sands, 7 April 1947. The winner (left) was T.H. Fenwick. On the right is Jack Hilton (aged 79) who had won 11 races over the last 15 years; he is wearing the same running shoes he had used on the track for the last 40 years.

Mr A. Pitt of Ushaw Moor (an older runner) was given an extra start in the young men's Easter Race on The Sands, 7 April 1947.

Cheery folk at The Sands, Easter Fair, 7 April 1947.

Staff working in the repair room at Lynch's radio shop, 30 North Road, April 1947.

The Durham High School playing field, originally Paradise Gardens (now part of the site of the Prince Bishop Shopping Centre), May 1947.

Children from Western Hill School at the opening of their annual concert, May 1947. The picture was taken next to the Obelisk in the grounds of St Leonard's RC School.

Mr Marshall, 'Cumberland Jack', enjoys a few moments outside his former home in Framwellgate, May 1947. It is interesting to see the stone foundations of an earlier building.

Lyon's Café, Silver Street, 23 May 1947, showing the ancient staircase. This property was once the town house of Sir John Duck, Durham's Dick Whittington, built c.1658. Later it became the Black Lion Hotel, then Caldcleugh's Ironmongers, and finally a café. The building was demolished in 1963 and replaced by a modern structure.

Mr Erik Brown, left, of Brown's Boathouse, presenting to the Regatta Committee a handsome cup in memory of his father, the late Mr Joseph Brown, June 1947. Erik's father had been the official university boat-builder since c.1903.

The funeral service of the Mayor, Councillor F. Foster, at St Cuthbert's Church, 28 May 1947. The cortège was led by a detachment of Durham County Constabulary. The Mayor's bodyguard and officers from the city council followed Councillor Foster had a long and distinguished career in the County Constabulary and entered the local council within a year of his retirement from the Police Force, about 1940.

Police competing for the Durham County Constabulary Golfing Trophy at Mount Oswald Golf Course, Durham, 9 June 1947. Competitors were Assistant Chief Constable J. Wright, Inspector H.W. Coyne, Supt. T.R. Hammond, Inspector J.J. Hugill, , PC H. Ross, PC R.M. Collinson and PC.Carr.

Brandon Colliery Welfare Flower Show and Sports Show, 30 August 1947, showing 'Zulu Warrior', Fred Hayton, of Brandon Colliery, and an unidentified 'old soldier', leading the procession. The show was attended by about 7,000 people. One of the events was a fancy dress parade with £1 being given to the person causing the most fun on the route.

The presentation of the Durham County Press Cups by Mr Arnold Rowntree at Durham Town Hall, 5 September 1947. Mr Charlton, Wheatley Hill, received a cup for the best display of chrysanthemums and the allotment cup; also the trophy for the best collection of vegetables, on behalf of Thornley Allotment Society. The cup for best display of honey went to Teesside Beekeepers' Association.

Above and right:
Spectators in the
Market Place at the
students annual 'Rag',
June 1947. Note the old
Police Box and granite
setts.

Durham Wasps, ice hockey team, October 1947. Back
row, left to right: Bill Britt, senior (Secretary), Joe
Stephenson (Ferryhill), Russ Proudfoot (Ferryhill),
Geordie Belmore (Darlington), Jim Hall (Hetton-le-
Hole), Chips Vine (Leamside), Bob Sandcaster
(Gateshead), Bob Thomp-
son (Bearpark), Butch
Cartwright (Pity Me), J.J.
Smith (Rink Manager) and
Bob Bruin (Whitley Bay).
Front row: Bill Britt, Junior,
George Gibson (Darling-
ton), Flash Lynn (Leamside),
Earl Carlson (Darlington)
and Mike Davy (Coach). The
photograph was taken prior
to the first British Ice
Hockey International Match
between an English and
Scottish team. The Wasps
played Kirkcaldy Flyers, the
score being 5-4 to Kirkcaldy.

The visit of Princess Elizabeth, 23 October 1947. This was her first visit to the city. She was here to lay the foundation stone for St Mary's new college. She began her journey to the college after visiting the Cathedral.

The Army recruitment office, 78 Claypath, December 1947. It is still operating from the same site.

1948

Jean Dodd, aged 11, of 48 Annand Road, is seen taking part in one of the first official ceremonies on the new Sunderland Road Estate, 18 January 1948. The tree was one of several silver birches planted. The Revd Dr E.G. Pace blessed the trees and offered prayers for the work of the Gardeners' Guild. He said everyone wanted the new houses to be not only places in which to eat and sleep, but to be real homes in which to take pride.

Children walking through ruined houses at Pittington, February 1948. Villagers were campaigning for new housing developments for the population of about 1,600. Many of the houses, which were still occupied, had been condemned.

Major General C.L. Loewen CB, GOC, 50th Division, inspecting men of the 8th Battalion, Durham Light Infantry, outside the Drill Hall, at the bottom of Gilesgate Bank, prior to the arrival of Mr E. Shinwell, Minister of War, March 1948. The Minister was touring the Northern Command to encourage staff officers in the drive for expansion of the TA. Officers present were, Lieut. Col G.L. Wood, DSO, MC, and Capt P.F. Greenwell, MC.

Soldiers standing to attention outside the 8th Battalion DLI Drill Hall, March 1948. Left to right: Privates Coxon and Kennedy, Sergeant Bainbridge, DCM, Privates Forster and Harrison and Corporal.Coxon.

'Friends of the hospital' day at Durham County Hospital, North Road, 9 March 1948. Visitors are inspecting the new sun balcony, which was made possible by the fund raising efforts of the Friends.

Student 'Rag', Palace Green, April 1948, showing a student claiming to be a Labour MP.

Pattison's Café, Old Elvet, April 1948, now part of the Royal County Hotel.

Belmont and St Oswald's Churches held an impressive service at Finchale Priory on Ascension Day, May 1948. St Oswald's choir led the procession, the Revd C. Pickles, vicar of St Mary Magdalene, Belmont, conducted the service, and the Revd L. Lloyd Rees, Chaplain of Durham Prison, preached the sermon.

Framwellgate Moor and Pity Me Homing Pigeon Society, May 1948. Seated, in the centre, is Jack Hird, a pigeon-flyer for 41 years.

About 9,000 pigeons being released at Durham Railway Station belonging to homing-pigeon societies from many parts of the country, 22 May 1948.

Durham Horse Fair, Old Elvet, 18 May 1948, showing Norman, Kenneth and Charlie Brown being driven by their cousin, Tommy Brown.

The Women's Labour Gala procession in North Road heading towards Wharton Park, photographed with Mr Hugh Dalton, MP for Bishop Auckland, who was one of the speakers, 5 June 1948.

Members of the Church Lads' Brigade on their way to the cathedral for their annual service, June 1948, photographed passing the Durham County Hospital, North Road.

The official opening of Langley Bridge Milk Factory, 4 June 1948. The Milk Marketing Board built it on a one and half acre site; it took nearly four years to build and equip. Milk was pasteurised here at a rate of 2,000 bottles an hour. The site is now vacant and awaiting redevelopment.

Father Meagher, conducting the opening service at Durham ice-rink, on the occasion of the second post-war Roman Catholic Gala, 2 August 1948. Between 4,000-5,000 people attended from all parts of the Diocese of Hexham and Newcastle. In the afternoon a great gathering enjoyed games and Irish dancing on The Racecourse.

Army Cadets, Air Training Corps and Sea Cadets outside the cathedral after their annual church parade, 26 September 1948.

Sea Rangers from Durham High School and St Oswald's Church attending the launch ceremony of their boat SRS *British Princess*. The Mayor, Councillor H.C. Ferens, seen at St Cuthbert's landing stage, christened it with lemonade, 8 October 1948. The crew consisted of Minnie Cook (coxswain), Pat Forgan, Madeleine Brown, Jean Urquart, Audrey Stobbs and Kathleen Surtees.

Many of the prize-winners belonging to Durham Commercial College, Victoria Terrace, photographed after receiving their awards at the speech day ceremony held in the Town Hall, November 1948.

Men making jackets as part of a tailoring course at Finchale Rehabilitation Centre, November 1948.

Father Christmas makes a special appearance at a party arranged by Durham Police, December 1948.

1949

A walking race from Coxhoe to Durham, 6 February 1949. The two competitors were Walter Salisbury and Jack Simpson. Simpson had a head start of two miles, moving off from the Hare & Greyhounds, Bowburn. Salisbury, who was the more experienced, won by five minutes; he is seen here entering New Elvet.

Mr Hugh Gaitskell, centre, Minister of Mines, with Mr J.D. Murray, MP accompanied by NCB officials on a visit to Brandon Pit House Colliery, March 1949. The minister had descended the shaft and crawled on his stomach to an 18" seam to talk to men at the coal-face. He wanted to see for himself the working conditions of the mine.

The 4th Durham (Gilesgate) Scouts on their 'Bob-a-job' tasks, assisting in the production of potato crisps. Baby-minding is performed by Jimmy Harris, April 1949. A total of £21 18s 5d was raised.

Durham County Fire Brigade on parade at The Sands, Durham, 23 May 1949. Twenty-six stations from the County took part and over 200 personnel assembled for the visit of HM Inspector of Fire Services, Mr P.P. Booth. The open space in the centre of the photograph is now the site of council flats.

John Pilkington from Gilesgate holding the pigeon, which won the Deerness Valley Federation Race from Brussels, June 1949.

A baptism ceremony at Finchale Abbey attended by several thousand young and old 'Ambassadors of Christ' (Pentecostal Church Assemblies of God. Many folk had made a pilgrimage to this sacred spot from all over the country by taxi, car, bicycle, bus and on foot, Whit Monday 6 June 1949. The ceremony was organised by Pastor N. Humphries of Houghton-le-Spring. Pastor Humphries and E.J. Shearman of Willington conducted the baptisms. Mr Joseph Speed of Newbottle, also known as 'Silver King' because of the colour of his hair, is seen before he went under the water. He told the crowd that his pipe and baccy were going with him and he would never smoke again.

Miss Gladys Coates of Durham School of Dancing, Mountjoy, with her pupils on the lawn of Bede College prior to their taking part in a display of dancing, 2 July 1949. One of her former pupils was the Prime Minister, Tony Blair. Miss Coates trained as a teacher of dancing in Newcastle and started the Durham School of Dancing in 1934-5. Her studio was built by her father, the builder, Tom Coates. She married Tommy Blair in 1940, and continued to use her maiden name for teaching purposes. From 1975 she was helped by her daughter, Jennifer, who continued to teach ballet, although the studio was closed when Miss Coates died in 1996.

George Bennett & Albert Wood in *Ice Capers* a spectacular show on ice, staged at Durham Ice Rink, 22 August 1949.

The opening of the 100th house at Sherburn Village by Councillor F. Kidd, Chairman of the Rural Council. The tenant was Mr G. Wilson of Pittington, 10 August 1949.

Durham City & District Bee Keeping Association's exhibit, which had gained a cup at the County Press & Houghall Show, September 1949. Houghall Show began in the 1930s during the depression, when thousands of miners were out of work. It was first held at Dryburn. After World War Two the *Durham County Press* established their own show in the Town Hall. The first joint show was held in 1948.

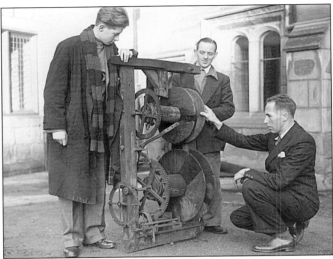

Remains of an ancient clock believed to date from around 1750, which was found by Mr W.W. Cope of Messrs G. & F. Cope of Nottingham in a small circular tower overlooking the quadrangle of Durham Castle, November 1949.

Prize winners at Bluecoat School, Claypath, December 1949.

Mine host Mr Jack Fallon (with the tray), at The Station Hotel, Leamside, photographed among his friends on his last night behind the bar, 28 November 1949. Those present were: Joseph Gibson, Tommy Peat, Charles Trott, Dick Harrison, E. McIlwraith, W. Morley, G. Gibson, Billy Kelly, W. Robinson, T. Storey, J. Appleby, F. Russell, W. Anderson and Bob Peebles.

Alderman J.W. Pattinson, JP (left), with some of the old folk of Elvet and Houghall, to whom he and Mrs Pattinson made an annual gift, December 1949. Alderman Pattinson was born in the city and educated first at the Wesleyan Day School and then later at the Bluecoat School. For about five years he was a footman at Durham Castle and Hatfield Hall. Later he became the proprietor of the Dunelm Hotel, Old Elvet. He was also a prominent soldier with the City Corps of the Salvation Army.

Participants in the Junior Contest of the Durham County Brass Band League, Junior Contest, which was, held at Gilesgate Welfare (Vane Tempest Hall), 1949. Photographed outside the old main entrance.

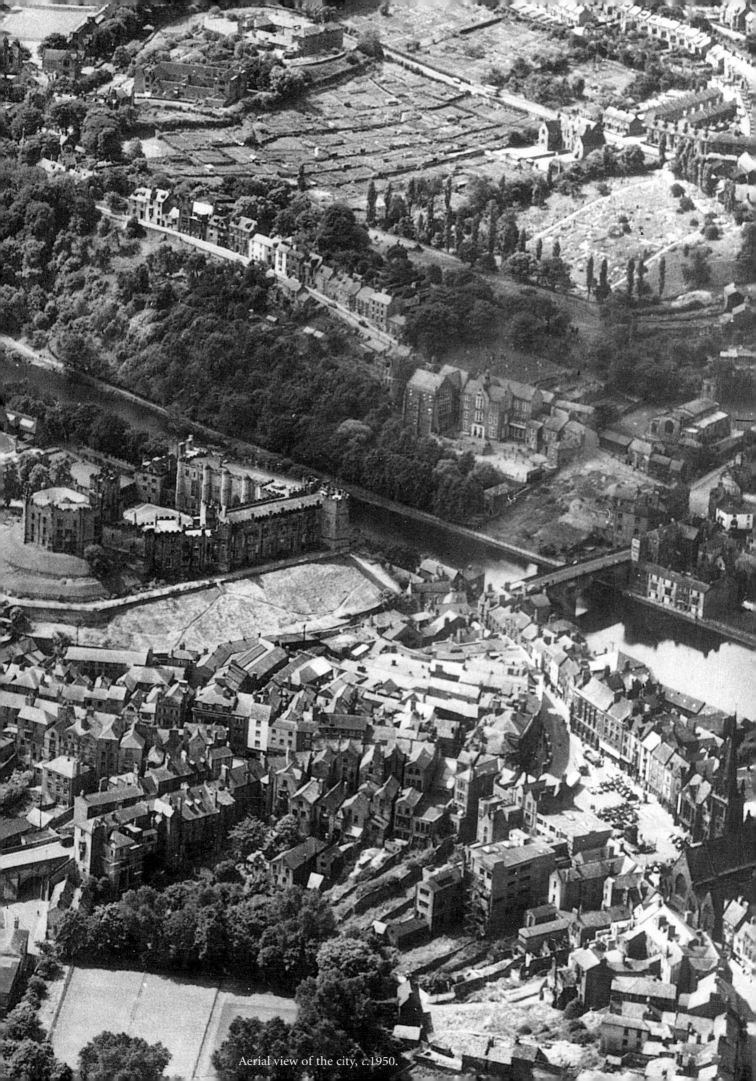

Aerial view of the city, *c.*1950.

1950

Mr Charles Frederick Grey, MP (Labour) photographed after his election, with supporters and family, outside the Town Hall, 24 February 1950. Mr Grey entered Parliament in 1945 and held the seat until 1970. He was born in 1904, and started work at the age of 14 at Elemore Colliery, where he worked for more than 20 years as a coal-hewer. A native of Easington Lane Mr Grey was a miners' lodge official before 1945, and also an Independent Methodist preacher.

Mackay's football team photographed before it was defeated 2-0 in the final of the Tudhoe Orphanage Cup at Spennymoor, April 1950. Back row, left to right: Walter Shea, Fred Wharton, Tommy Little, Bobby Noble, Jack Wade, Billy Wardle and Wilf Helm. Front row, left to right: Joss Milburn, Charlie McArdle, Jimmy Crampton, George Wood and Bob Bell.

Sir Robert Chapman DL took the salute when 3,000 Boy Scouts attended a St George's Day parade and service at Durham Cathedral, 23 April 1950. The Bishop of Jarrow, the Revd J.A. Ramsbotham, preached the sermon.

The Galilee Chapel, Durham Cathedral, showing members of the Durham County Fellowship of Religion, prior to their presentation of 'The Figure on the Cross', 13 May 1950.

Rogation Day procession from St Oswald's Church, May 1950. It is seen winding its way through Thorndyke (also known as Klondike) Allotments where the crops were blessed. The procession is led by Crucifer, Mr F.Kny-Jones. This area is now part of the university science site on Stockton Road.

One of Durham's young dancing instructors, Pauline Chamberlain, with her pupils after a display in the Town Hall, 17 May 1950. Pauline was 17 years of age when she opened her dancing school in 1947 and it continued until she retired in 1970.

The new Chancellor of the University of Durham Dr G.M. Trevelyan (third from the right) leads the procession from the castle to the cathedral, with Sir James Duff (second from the right), May 1950.

Mr L.O. Duncan, a Somerset journalist, and his wife, were on a caravan tour of Great Britain, June 1950. They are photographed visiting Durham where they were met by the Mayor, Councillor H.H. Rushford, and Miss Gwen Wilkinson, (representing the RSPCA). The caravan was drawn up in the grounds of Durham Moor Farm. While on the journey, Mr Duncan was writing a book about his adventure.

Members from Neville's Cross Social club outside the club, prior to their outing to Bamburgh and Seahouses, 25 June 1950.

Odd-job man, Thomas Robinson, aged 70, a retired builder's labourer, photographed pointing the boundary wall of the bowling green which he had built at Gilesgate Welfare (Vane Tempest Hall), July 1950.

The Gilesgate Welfare Association Friendly Circles' first birthday, at Vane Tempest Hall, July 1950. Miss Moore, aged 83, cuts the cake, watched by the vicar of St Giles's, Canon Jack Norwood.

The Shakespeare Band's 'big drummer' keeps time as his colleagues entertain spectators at Durham City AFC's, first home game. The match took place on The Racecourse, 2 September 1950.

Boer War veteran, Tommy Nevison of Bishop Auckland, taking aim, at the Durham Light Infantry Association's reunion which was held at Brancepeth Castle, 31 September 1950. This was the 17th annual reunion of the DLI Regimental Association.

The 'Free Orchard' near The Sands, October 1950. Officials discussing plans for the new sports stadium for Durham City AFC, which was to be built on the site. Members of the group are: left to right: J.P. Carswell (assistant secretary), Walter Stones, B. Caldcleugh, Jack Holloway and Raymond Appleby (chairman).

Mr Justice Hallett (right) and Mr Justice Finnemore attending a service at the cathedral with the Mayor, Councillor Mrs H.H. Rushforth, and members of the Corporation, 22 October 1950. Also in the group are Dean Alington (rear left) and Mr J.K. Hope, Recorder (front left).

The master of the Durham County Foxhounds, greeting children near Shincliffe School, at the beginning of a meet, November 1950.

Flooded bus-stands when the Wear broke its banks in Framwellgate, November 1950. The young boy is Robert Howe. Note the bus going over Framwellgate Bridge.

A brightly-painted bus belonging to the Express Omnibus Co. (Durham) Ltd., Palace Green, November 1950. The firm was established at Gilesgate Moor in the 1930s.

Youth organisations of Durham Division Salvation Army demonstrating their activities at an exhibition in Durham Town Hall, 2 December 1950. More than 500 young soldiers crowded into the Town Hall.

A Christmas party at Millburngate Nursery School, December 1950. The building stood on part of the site of the present Millburngate shopping centre.

Sorting the Christmas post at Durham Post Office, Claypath, December 1950. The post office building was opened in 1929, after the one in Saddler Street closed. It has now been converted into private apartments.

A magician pulls a rabbit out of a hat for children at a Christmas party organised by Durham Police, December 1950.

1951

Durham County Federation of Young Farmers' ploughing champion, Alan Kingston, son of Councillor J. Kingston, Hallgarth Farm, Elvet, 13 January 1951. Alan had won the contest for 21-24 year olds, held at Mount Huley Farm, Ferryhill.

The British Legion women of Pittington gave a treat to the village children by arranging for them to see a talking movie provided by the National Savings Committee, January 1951.

Sherburn Village Co-operative football team photographed outside the Grey Horse public house, Sherburn, after its victory with Stanley NGT, in the Durham Mid-Week Cup Replay, February 1951. Back row, left to right: G. Travis, unknown, R. Beckworth, unknown and G. Walters. Front row: A.Leonard, T. Watson, T. Coates, G. Harding, R. Close, Billy Cooper and G. Blacklock. The landlord, John Walters, and his wife are looking out from the window.

The christening and launching of the 'Johnstonian' on the River Wear by Miss V.L. Gray, Chief Ministry of Education Inspector, Durham area, 9 February 1951. On the right wearing the glasses, is Mr Donald Webster, Vice-Principal of Bede College. The boat had been built by 10 pupils from the school under the direction of the woodwork master, Mr A. Kirkman. On the left are the crew, Alan Shea, Jim Harris and Ian Shepherd.

Smiling Sherburn United FC officials, outside the Lambton Arms public house, Sherburn Hill, prior to the County Amateur Cup match with Wheatley Hill's team which defeated them by 5-1, 17 February 1951.

A wagon carrying bales of hay, seen after it had overturned, near the Magdalen Steps, Saddler Street, March 1951. It is thought that the driver had driven up Saddler Street by mistake. On his return, instead of heading towards the Market Place to turn around the Police Box, he seems to have attempted to make an illegal move, turning right onto Elvet Bridge.

Alison Margaret, aged 19 months, the daughter of the Chief Constable, A.A. Muir, at her front gate on Potters' Bank, Durham City, April 1951.

Her Royal Highness the Princess Margaret in her capacity of sea Ranger Commodore, May 1951. She is photographed on Palace Green on the occasion of her visit to inspect the Girl Guides and Sea Rangers of the County.

Almost 5,000 Guides and Rangers assembled on Palace Green, May 1951. After the Princess left the saluting base she spoke to those girls who had collapsed during the parade.

To mark the advent of women into Durham City Council, citizens started a public subscription for a portrait of the first woman Mayor, Councillor Hannah Harrison Rushford, April 1951. Mr T.W. Pattison, a well-known Newcastle artist, carried out the commission

The laying up ceremony at Durham Cathedral of the banner of the Durham City Branch of the Old Contemptibles, 29 April 1951. The banner, which was dedicated in 1934, by the Dean of Durham, was handed over at the start of evensong to Dean Alington, who said: 'Most gladly I receive the banner into the custody of the cathedral'. It was recently found discarded and it is now displayed in Durham Heritage Centre and Museum, North Bailey.

Col. Sir Robert Chapman presenting a cheque for £1,000 to Dr Alington, a gift of appreciation from the people of Durham County upon his retirement after 18 years, May 1951. He and his wife, the Hon. Hester Alington, moved to Herefordshire on retirement.

The County Festival of Youth, held at Hollow Drift, 2 June 1951, more than 5,000 people attended. There were numerous demonstrations and displays by 87 organisations. In the background is seen the water tower and signal cabin belonging to Elvet Railway Station.

Billy Smart's Circus at The Sands, 9 July 1951. The elephant was Birma, aged nine, who had made several television appearances. She was part of a competition to guess her weight, the winner receiving a free ticket for the show.

Mr Sam Watson, left, representing the Durham Miners' Association, and Mr E.H.D. Skinner, the National Coal Board, make their way to the cathedral for the Easington Colliery Memorial Service, July 1951.

Durham Women's Labour Gala (started in 1923), 9 June 1951. The photograph shows Pelaw Ward banner and Councillor Wilf Edge (centre), outside the Royal County Hotel, Old Elvet. The day was marred with the news of the Easington Colliery disaster.

The rolled-up banner of Easington Colliery being carried towards the cathedral, followed by Easington Public Band, for the memorial service, July 1951, The Easington Colliery disaster had happened on 29 May 1951, 83 men (including two rescue-workers) lost their lives. Over 4,000 people crowded into the cathedral for the sombre service.

The Easington Colliery banner, unfurled and draped in black, leaving the cathedral after the memorial service, July 1951.

The installation of Dean Wild in the cathedral, 11 October 1951. Standing, left to right: Archdeacon Lucas, Canon Richardson, Professor Turner and Professor Greenslade. Seated, left to right: The Very Revd J.H.S. Wild, Dr Williams, the Bishop of Durham and the Rt. Revd J.A. Ramsbotham, the Bishop of Jarrow.

Farmer Bill Hopps, who provided the turf for the playing area at Durham City's new football ground, 13 October 1951. He had the honour of kicking the ball off to start the first match against Sunderland 'A' team. Unfortunately Durham didn't celebrate the event with a win, but lost 3-2.

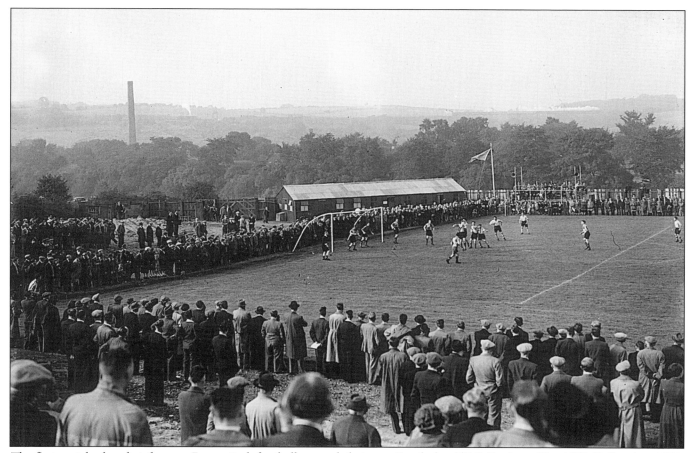

The first match played at the new Ferens Park football ground, between Sunderland 'A' & Durham City AFC, 13 October 1951.

Straight from preaching his first sermon since his installation, the new Dean, the Very Revd J.H.S. Wild, was photographed with the choristers in the Cloister Garth, 14 October 1951.

The unveiling of the stained glass window in Durham Town Hall by the Colonel of the Regiment, Brigadier I.A. Churchill, November 1951. It commemorated the honour bestowed on the Durham Light Infantry on 15 March 1944, of marching through the city with bayonets fixed and colours uncased.

After a lapse of 20 years, greyhound coursing was revived at Low Carr House Farm, near Framwellgate Moor. Farmer T. Turnbull and a few 'hopefuls' held a private meeting to see if there was likely to be support, December 1951.

1952

An aerial view of the Geography Department (right) and the Dawson Building, opened 1924 (centre left), Stockton Road, c.1952. Bottom left corner is the New Inn at the head of Church Street.

Edwin Thomas, aged 29, of High Street, Carrville (right), and James Glaister, aged 18, of Millburngate, had a lucky escape when the roof they were working on in The College collapsed, sending 40 tons of lime stone slates crashing to the ground, 7 January 1952. It was the home of Mrs M.J. Burton, widow of the late George Burton, Head Verger.

Thirteen-year-old Norman Davis of Ludworth the youngest member of Durham Model Flying Club, January 1952. He is seen demonstrating to youngsters who visited an exhibition of models at The Palladium Cinema, Claypath.

The 'Tuesday Club', Gilesgate Welfare Association (Vane Tempest Hall), January 1952. Star of the BBC Radio show, 'Wot Cheor, Geordie', Bobby Thompson, meets the ladies. Back row, second from the left, is Sally Savage, and fourth from the left, is Margaret Clark, née Savage.

Window displays by Mackay's Carpets at Sawrey Gill's shop, 102-104 Claypath, March 1952. Martha Stewart is pictured sewing. The shop was then situated at the bottom of Claypath opposite St Nicholas' Church.

Durham Press Ball at the Princess Ballroom in the Three Tuns Hotel, New Elvet, March 1952. Guest of the Durham & District Journalists, was Alec Guinness (left) 300 newspapermen and their friends attended from all over the north-east. The man on the right, wearing the bow tie is Albert Birch of Musgrave Gardens.

Members of Durham County Auxiliary Fire Service (AFS) practising at Finchale Abbey, 19 April 1952.

Alderman W. McKeag, Lord Mayor of Newcastle (a native of Belmont), photographed after he had preached from the pulpit of Belmont Parish Church, 27 April 1952. The occasion was Industrial Sunday.

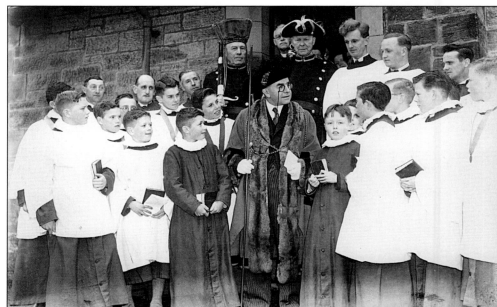

Victorious Newcastle United halted at Durham Railway Station on its way home, May 1952. Team Capt. Joe Harvey, left, de-trained to let the young folk have a look at the famous trophy. On the right is team-mate Frank Brennan.

Mr C.F. Grey, MP (centre), unveiling a new banner for the Pelaw Ward Labour Party Women's Section, June 1952. It shows the portrait of the city councillor for the ward Wilf Edge, who is on the left.

While on a visit to the city, the Hon. Mrs Hester Alington (wife of the former Dean) met old friends at Alington House Youth Club, North Bailey, June 1952. Guides and Brownies soon made her feel at home again.

Guests at the garden party in the grounds of St Margaret's Vicarage, June 1952. Left to right: The Deputy Mayoress, Mrs Rae, Canon Thurlow, Miss Thurlow and the Mayoress, Mrs Gordon McIntyre.

Crowds gather in the Market Place to see soldiers from the 1st Battalion Durham Light Infantry before they left for Korea, 20 July 1952. The streets from Old Elvet to the Market Place were lined five deep with well-wishers.

Top: The cobbled streets of
Durham City echoed to the sound
of marching feet, when the County
bade farewell to the 1st Battalion
Durham Light Infantry, 20 July
1952. It was to sail for Korea at the
end of July. The soldiers were
photographed on their way to a
special farewell service at the
cathedral. Afterwards a book of
remembrance was dedicated
containing the names of 3,000
men of the regiment who gave
their lives in World War Two.

Middle: The window of the army
recruitment office, 78 Claypath,
advertising the film *Rommel –
Desert Fox*, starring James Mason, 2
July 1952. The film was being
shown at the Majestic Cinema,
Sherburn Road.

Bottom: Oak mayoral chairs and
prayer-book-stands made by
Gradons, North Road, August
1952. They are seen in the
workshops, prior to their delivery
to the cathedral. They were the gift
of Alderman H.L. Gradon, JP, and
were made by his craftsmen, the
names of whom are carved on the
bottom of the chairs. They were
formally handed over and
dedicated, 5 October 1952.

The Mayor and Mayoress Councillor and Mrs Gordon McIntyre at the opening of the seventh annual vegetable and flower show, which was held at Gilesgate Welfare Association (Vane Tempest Hall), 4 August 1952. They are photographed with the President of the Association, Mr W. McIntyre (right). Over 1,000 people had attended the event.

The Mayor and Mayoress, Councillor and Mrs Gordon McIntyre, addressing the first parcel from the Korean Comforts Fund, to Pte. M. Appleby, who was serving in Korea with the Durham Light Infantry, 26 September 1952.

Belmont motorcycle scrambles, September 1952. The area has now become a nature conservation site. The railway is the Sherburn to Carrville stretch of the Leamside line.

The 'Red Devils', County Paratroopers of the 17th Battalion (9th DLI) TA rehearsing for the royal visit of HRH Princess Royal at Brancepeth Castle, October 1952. The Princess was arriving on the 4 October to present new colours.

Inspector G.W. Spencer, RSPCA, and Mrs E.M. Minto carried these swans to the River Wear at Durham, and set them free, October 1952. They had been rescued at Wingate earlier in the day; their wings had been clipped.

A milk tanker, which had crashed outside Bow School, at the bottom of South Road, was carrying 1,700 gallons, December 1952. Lance Ford, and his three-year-old son Bill are on the right.

Councillor Wilf Edge, Keeper of the Wheel of fortune at St Joseph's Christmas fair, Mill Lane, Gilesgate, December 1952. Father Meagher and Father Kenny are in front of the wheel; about £400 was raised.

1953

George Lye of Fillinghams, Elvet Bridge, *c.*1953. George was a keen ice-hockey player with the Durham Wasps, as well as being a professional photographer. He is well remembered for his service to Durham through his business, Fillingham's Photography.

Field Marshal Viscount Montgomery's visit to Durham to receive the Freedom of the City, 14 January 1953. He became the 16th Honorary Freeman of the City.

Durham students' 'Rag', February 1953. 'West Point soldiers', armed with mops, giving the road a spring clean, as they come over Framwellgate Bridge towards North Road.

'The West Point soldiers' and their minders, part of the university 'Rag', near the County Hospital, February 1953.

Schoolgirls v Factory Girls', March 1953. Whinney Hill girls (with sashes) were guests of girls employed at Wood & Watson ('pop' factory), Gilesgate in a game of netball. The schoolgirls won 12-9.

Wood & Watsons' football team, photographed before it was defeated 4-1 by Mackays' carpet factory team, March 1953. Back row, left to right: Tommy Rowntree, Billy Lish, George Holt, John Coulthard, Alan Proudlock and Billy Corbett. Front row: Tommy Tempest, Alan Brooks, Alan Robson, Ronnie Barker, unknown, Jackie Chapelow and Reggie Lee.

Finalists in the Durham St Margaret's billiards and snooker competition, April 1953. The players are, left to right: Norman Foster, Robert Metcalf, George Snowball and Bill Sones. The trophies are the C.J. Thurlow Snooker Trophy (left), and the Ralph Watson Billiards Cup (right).

Mr Nelson Rouse of the Neville Dene Hotel, Crossgate Moor (now The Pot & Glass), packing away the dyed eggs after an Easter competition, April 1953. The leek club savings group had decided to send the eggs to children at Earl's House Hospital.

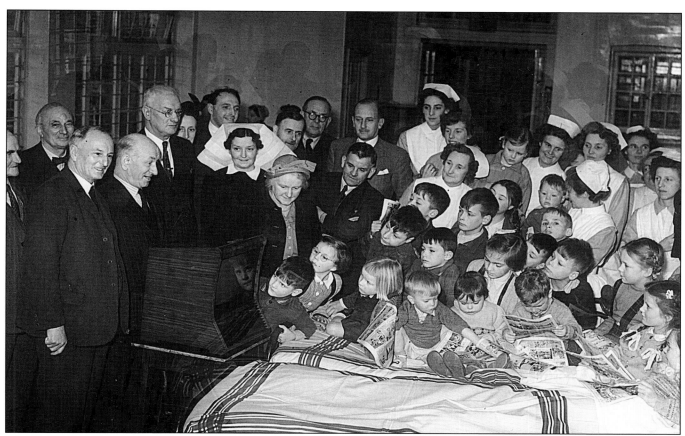

The presentation of a television set for Earl's House Hospital, the gift of the TV Comic, April 1953. The Mayor and Mayoress Councillor & Mrs G. McIntyre, Alderman J.W. Foster, County Councillor G. Dowsey and Mr and Mrs A. Bewick attended the presentation, where the children showed great excitement.

Children of Shincliffe Church of England School attending a ceremony at which a number of Coronation Trees were planted, May 1953.

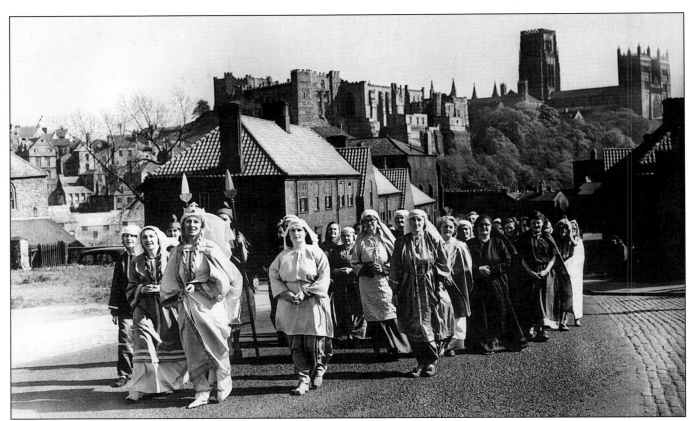

Durham Catholic Women's League photographed in Framwellgate, after rehearsing an episode from 'Queen Elizabeth', which they were to perform in a pageant, at Newcastle City Hall, May 1953.

Mr Oliver Hopkins, 53 Musgrave Gardens, 1 June 1953, with the original Griffin which had been made for King George V, 31 years before, by Mr F. Minto of London. The Griffin originally stood on a turret on St George's Chapel, Windsor. It was used as part of Mr Hopkin's decorations in honour of Queen Elizabeth's Coronation.

An unidentified group at their coronation party, Gilesgate Welfare (Vane Tempest Hall), June 1953.

The baby daughter of Mr and Mrs Lily Brooks, 98 Bradford Crescent, Gilesgate. They had won the prize awarded to the baby born nearest to midnight on Coronation Eve, June 1953. Baby Hilary is photographed on her mother's knee with the Mayor and Mayoress, Councillor and Mrs J.R. Kingston, holding the prizes, a basket and shawl.

Durham County Press tour of London. 300 County Durham people went to London for 12 hours to view the coronation decorations, 18 May 1953. Photographed after watching the Changing of the Guard at Buckingham Palace.

After taking passengers to a cricket match at Old Durham Gardens, this double-decker bus had an unfortunate accident on the return journey, June 1953. It was carrying spectators who had been watching a match between a Sunderland team and the North Eastern Social and Cultural Organisation for the Blind. Thirty people were injured, including several children; one man was detained in the County Hospital. Note the letters on the destination panel, 'SCT' (Sunderland Corporation Transport).

A contingent of Methodists from Framwellgate Moor, in procession towards the cathedral for the Methodist 'Big Meeting', where over 2,000 attended the service, 27 July 1953. It was their 7th annual Big Meeting.

The proceeds from the Durham County Hospital Football Competition were used to purchase a television set which was installed in Ward 1 of Durham County Hospital, July 1953. The group shows: Alderman J. Foster, Mr Ralph Smith, Mr T. Lawson, Dr G. Byrne and Miss M.G. Harding (Matron) at the presentation.

The annual rally of No.7 Group of the British Legion, 12 July 1953. The rally was held in the Town Hall instead of The Racecourse due to the heavy rain. The photograph shows the women's section in the Market Place.

Members of Durham Rugby Club, 5 September 1953. The club president Councillor J. Turnbull, presented 80 inscribed silver tankards (the largest number ever awarded) to the players, who had set up a record the previous season when winning five trophies.

Vandalism at the County War Memorial in the North Bailey, September 1953. The memorial stands outside the east end of the cathedral under the rose window. It commemorates men of the county who were killed in World War One. It was unveiled by the Lord Lieutenant, the Marquess of Londonderry, 24 November 1928.

The first official leader of Durham City Baptist Church, Miss Freda Buckley (centre), meeting some of the congregation who attended her ordination and induction, in the 'Hut', Edward Street, Gilesgate, October 1953. Top left, left to right: Brian Nichols, Mrs Nichols (snr), Mrs Anita Nicholls and Mary Walker.

Sherburn Road Youth Centre, 2 November 1953. Members of the Evergreen Club for spinsters, widows and aged people at their first birthday party. Mrs E. Oliver cuts the cake, with the Revd Jack Norwood, Vicar of St Giles's Church.

Scholars from Brandon Modern School presenting a Christmas nativity play in aid of Brancepeth Village Church, 750th Anniversary restoration appeal, 3 December 1953. It was produced by Mr R. Naylo and the music was conducted by Miss L. Raine. Names of those taking part were: Brian Strong, Jean Stoker, Neville Thompson, Brian Derbyshire, Thomas Richardson, Donald Reavley, Ronald Best, Edwin Evans, Tony Eales, Barbara Seed, Isabel Ward, Margaret Anderson, Margaret Kennedy, Lorna Maddison and Aileen Wright.

A city council employee attaches a line to the life-saving belt at Pelaw Wood, November 1953. The council was beginning to get tired of renewing this particular line as it was frequently disappearing (being stolen for washing lines).

The Revd Jack Norwood, Vicar of St Giles's Church, serving ice cream at the church bazaar, which was held in the old church hall (now the site of St Giles's petrol station), November 1953.

1954

A collection point for the Prisoners' Aid Fund appeal at the Essoldo picture-house, North Road, January 1954.

Student 'Rag', February 1954, showing the float from St Hild's College with the theme 'Infant Classroom'. The wagon, on loan from Wood & Watson's 'Pop' factory, Gilesgate, is seen outside the University Library on Palace Green.

The Palladium Cinema (left and middle), 26 Claypath, 26 February 1954. It was built by F.W. Goodyear and was opened, 18 March 1929, with Rex Ingram's, great new production, *The Garden of Allah*, with an all-star cast including Alice Terry and Ivan Retrovich. In the 1970s it became a bingo hall and for the last 20 years has remained empty, apart from a brief opening for a live screening of Billy Graham the Evangelist's visit to the North-East in the early 1980s.

Durham's 'Museum Pub', the Big Jug, Claypath, showing on the left, the landlord, Harry Callow, who was moving to a hotel at Hunwick, March 1954. His collectibles were up for sale, due to his new surroundings not being able to accommodate his old-world furniture. The lady is his 80-year-old mother.

Charmian Welsh (first in line) of Thornley, Durham's, 16-year-old Olympic diver, a member of Durham ASC, April 1954. She is photographed with the other seven contestants who were competing for the women's one-metre National Springboard Diving Championship that was being held at the city baths. This was the first time this international event was held at Durham. She retained her title by a comfortable margin.

Sir Cuthbert & Lady Headlam, photographed on the day of their golden wedding anniversary, at their residence, Holywell Hall, near Brancepeth Village, 27 April 1954. Henry, the cockatoo, who had been with them for over 37 years, also joined in with the celebrations.

'Dowager Duchess of the Sty' Moncur Lily, 5th Prize Pedigree dam of the Quarrington Herd of G. & W. Adamson, 18 May 1954. She was purchased from the famous Winterton Herd for 110 guineas, 17 of her grandchildren were also sold at the auction.

The Ven. J.O. Cobhan, Archdeacon of Durham, blessing the Church Army van outside the north door of the cathedral, after a rally to mark five years' work in the diocese of Durham, 22 May 1954. In the evening an open-air witness was held in Durham Market Place.

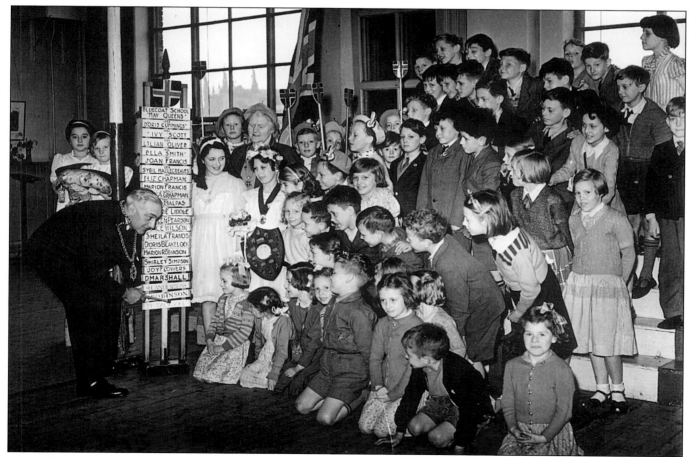

Councillor J.R. Kingston adds the May Queen's name to the list of former elected queens (from 1933). The pupils had elected Margaret Jackson, of Pittington, 24 May 1954. This was the last official duty of the Mayor before his term of office finished.

'The Towers', The Avenue, Durham City, June 1954. This was the former home of Dr F.F.T. Hare, and was bought by the hospital authorities to provide a training centre for nurses. The sister tutor was Mrs E. Gascoigne, who was in charge of the school with Miss M. Dingmole-Smith of Dryburn Hospital. Names of nurses in the group are: Joan Williams, Nora Rivers, June Cleghorn, Joy Larkin, Joan Waterson, Olwin Ridley, Hazel Fordy, Mary Wade, Pat Hogarth, Theresa Forster, Oliver Perry and Freda Spottiswood.

Red Cross Cadets, (leader, Mrs Berriman), who were enrolled at Gilesgate Welfare Association (Vane Tempest Hall) by Mrs Keardon, 21 June 1954. Names taking part were: Margaret Banks, Pamela Fowler, Christine Hindle, Brenda Hutchinson, Hazel Newton, Jill Percy, Pamela Rogers, Barbara Smith, Edith Barton, Jean Griffiths, Gladys Jackson, Margaret Hancock, Jennifer Parkin, Jean Ritson, Patricia Saynor, Roberta Storey and Tom Bartle. Junior Cadets pictured are: Elspeth Allan, Jennifer Allan, Elizabeth Berriman, Christine Bonner, Margaret Callan, Margaret Dempsey, Rosalind Gascoigne, Christine Gibson, Edna Hawkins, June Storey and Barbara Whyte. First aid certificates were presented to: Elizabeth Alderson, Nora Clark, Brian Fenwick, John Hedley, Doris Johnson, Vera Leggett, Keith Mawson, Joan Ramshaw, Sylvia Robertson, Peter Teggert and Len Wilson.

Mr Robert Mole, one of Durham's best known personalities, meets Mrs Bessie Braddock, MP at the Labour Women's Gala. He receives her autograph outside the Dun Cow public house, Old Elvet, 3 July 1954.

The Very Revd Canon G.P. Pippet, the beloved parish priest of St Godric's RC Church photographed with some of the children at St Godric's School, Castle Chare, as they celebrate his 50th years in the priesthood, July 1954.

Mr R. Gleason at Gilesgate Welfare Flower and Vegetable Show, Vane Tempest Hall, with his prize roses, 2 August 1954. Back (centre) with the trilby hat, is Herbie Ingram. Below him is Harry Bond with Florence McArdle on his right.

The veterans' race at Belmont Greyhound Stadium, August 1954. Billy Jones (centre) leads the field. On the outside rails is Charlie Ashworth, who won the photo finish against Billy Jones.

Maintenance man George Colwell, of 113 Gilesgate, aged 67, working at Durham brickworks, Sidegate, August 1954. The Durham Brick & Tile Works were established in the early 1930s by Alderman T.W. Holiday and were later managed by his two nephews, R. & L. Forrester.

Carpet examiners at Mackay's Carpet Factory, October 1954.

Durham Colleges' golf match at Brancepeth showing players who took part in the half-yearly staff v students match for the Gray-Rackham Trophy, December 1954. Seated in the centre is the Vice-Chancellor, Sir James Duff; on his left is Mr J. Gray, staff team captain.

1955

Brenda Atterton and Tom Willey, on the left, receive the President's Trophy from the Revd J. Norwood, after winning the Durham St Giles's Badminton Club Pairs Tournament, January 1955. Behind the vicar is Jean Reed.

Jazz enthusiasts, at a candle-lit scene in St Godric's Church Hall, Durham, 21 February 1955. Blaring trumpets introduced the first jazz session of this newly-formed club which was to 'ignite' every Monday during 1950 'jive'.

Young sledgers on the Observatory Field, near Durham School, February 1955.

Durham's smiling postman, Mr J.T. McClurg, senior postman at Durham Head Office, March 1955. He was photographed at Durham Railway Station on his last working day. (He joined the service in 1909.)

Right: Mr and Mrs T.E. Brown celebrated their golden wedding at the anvil of T.E. Brown & Son, Blacksmiths, Walkergate, 23 April 1955. He was one of the few remaining craftsmen left in the city. He was born in Meadowfield, served his apprenticeship in the city and later took up employment at Brandon Colliery. During World War One he served with the Army Veterinary Corps. He started his business in the city in 1926. It is now run by a grandson.

A judo display in the courtyard of Gilesgate Welfare Association (Vane Tempest Hall) one of the events from the programme of the Community Centre's Spring Festival, April 1955.

'Eyes Down' at the bingo stand, Easter Monday, on The Sands, April 1955.

Whit Monday, sailing on the River Wear, 23 May 1955.

Mr Harry Appleton and his staff from Shincliffe School returning from a nature lesson in the school's delightful surroundings, May 1955. The children were encouraged to preserve the beauty of their village by planting flowers and protecting trees.

History was made at Durham Baths, when 17-year-old Miss Charmian Welsh was granted the Freedom of the Baths for life, 23 May 1955. In the presence of the Mayor and Mayoress Councillor and Mrs H.L. Cawood, and other members of the Corporation, she was presented with a certificate by Alderman Pattison. She was the first person ever to receive this honour, a tribute to her outstanding achievements in competitive diving.

Members of the Women's Labour Gala procession, walking over Elvet Bridge, June 1955. They came from all parts of the County for their 32nd annual Gala at Wharton Park. The procession had started at Elvet Station and 11 bands took part.

Church Army Crusaders parade past the Right Revd A.M. Ramsey, Bishop of Durham following a ceremony at the cathedral, 4 July 1955. About 70 men and women were commissioned to visit seaside resorts all over the country.

St Margaret's School, Durham, July 1955. The picture was taken on the eve of the retirement of Miss Margaret Taylor, headmistress of the infants' school for 27 years, and Mr G. Sanderson who had taught for 35 years in the junior school. Gerry Steinberg, who later became MP for Durham City, is fifth from the left on the back row.

The last ceremony of the 2nd Battalion DLI before it was disbanded, 10 July 1955. Two old veterans of World War One, Mr A. Lawrence of Page Bank and Mr H. Henderson of Crook, are seen leaving the cathedral after a special service.

Mr Tom Owens of 63 Whinney Hill, Durham, photographed on his final shift, before retirement as an engine-driver, July 1955. Born in Durham he went to St Oswald's School until he was 13, then went to a local laundry and followed that up with a spell in a butcher's shop. Eventually, at the age of 16, he began work at Durham Station as a cleaner in 1906, his wage being 10s a week. He worked his way up to become a fireman and, after a serving with the DLI during World War One, he returned and trained as an engine-driver.

The news quickly spread after Barry Juniper caught a 6lbs pike in this pond at Pittington. Other hopefuls, wanting to try their luck, soon assembled, August 1955.

Two damaged vehicles at the junction of Whitesmocks Avenue. Both accidents occurred at almost the same spot within a few hours of each other, 29 August 1955.

Mr Bill Lane, British Legion car park attendant, aged 65, September 1955. He had been deaf, dumb and blind after being injured in the second battle of Ypres in December 1916, while serving with the 2nd & 13th DLI. He had also seen action at Hill 60, Vimy Ridge, Armentiers and the first battle of Ypres. After years of treatment his faculties were partly restored.

A torchlight procession was held starting in Milburngate, and going via North Road, and then to Wharton Park. There the annual camp-fire and singsong was attended by over 200 Durham and District Boy Scouts, and Girl Guides, 30 September 1955. The Mayoress, Mrs H.L. Cawood, lit the camp-fire, which was followed by the grand singsong.

Mr Nicholas Nimneys, of Framwellgate Moor, a former feather-weight boxer, photographed on his last day as a ticket-puncher at Durham Railway Station, October 1955. He had started his career on the railway as a plate-layer in 1922 and became a ticket-collector in 1942.

The Great Hall, Durham Castle, showing the luncheon-party, which was given for the American Ambassador, prior to a ceremony at Washington Old Hall, October 1955.

Mrs Agnes Tindale, Brancepeth Village's oldest resident, photographed at the village bazaar with her bran-tub, October 1955. The event was in aid of Brancepeth Church restoration fund.

Vandalism on Palace Green, after an attack by students from the Newcastle Division of Durham University, October 1955.

Mrs Mary Jenkins gives a 'penny for the guy' photographed in Annand Road, Gilesgate, 3 November 1955. Churchill flats are seen in the background. Left to right: Alan Dickson, Tony Greaves, Eddie Jenkins, Alan Greaves, Peter Hughes and Vic Richardson.

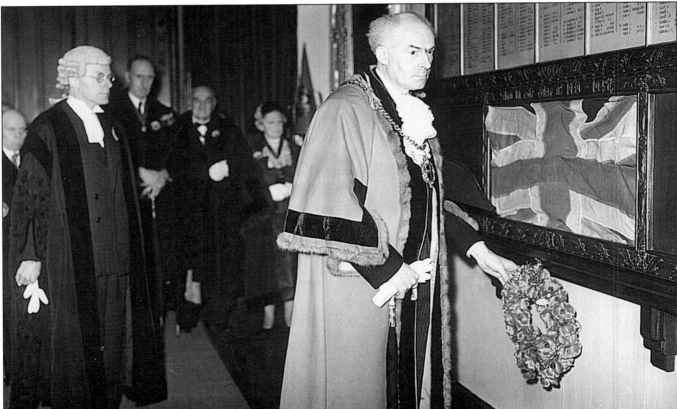

The Mayor, Councillor H.L. Cawood, at the Town Hall war memorial, on Remembrance Day, 11 November 1955. The memorial was designed by Mr E.J. Miles. The work was carried out by Mr James Lyons, and Mr W.G. Footitt executed the engrossing of the names. It was unveiled on 2 March 1921.

1956

Puss in Boots, performed by the Girls' Friendly Society at St Aidan's Church Hall, Framwellgate Moor, January 1956. Left to right: Dorothy Clarke, Linda Burrows, Carol Homes, unknown, unknown, unknown, Joan Lowes and Brian Exley. Seated is Joan Darwin.

An interior view of Archibald's 'Jagal House', North Road, on the day of its official opening, February 1956. It was designed by Cordingley and McIntyre, and was built by Holst and Co. Ltd. This was a very useful shop which stocked a wide variety of goods.

John Chapman of Annand Road, photographed with his collie dog, at the Gilesgate Canine Training Club, which was held at Vane Tempest Hall, May1956. His collie had won the trophy for best-conditioned dog. The president, Mr Sydney Wood (of Wood & Watson's 'Pop' factory), presented the trophy.

Some of the 70 members of Gilesgate Canine Training Club, May 1956. In the background are St Giles's Church, Wood & Watson's factory and Gilesgate Nursery School.

Fowler & Armstrong's garage, New Elvet, April 1956. On the top right is the Court Inn, Court Lane. Orchard House flats now occupy the site of the garage.

Hatfield students taking part in events organised as part of Hatfield Day, May 1956. The modern houses behind the crowd, are Hatfield View council houses, which were later demolished to make way for Elvet Riverside lecture theatre.

This view from Pelaw Wood, shows four popular Durham sports on The Racecourse; tennis, bowls, cricket and rowing, 26 May 1956. In the distance can been seen the old iron bridge belonging to Elvet Railway Station.

Durham Regatta crowds, 20 June 1956. On the evening of the last day of the Regatta hundreds gathered on The Racecourse for a spectacular firework display. Durham Amateur Rowing Club won two of the trophies during the two-day event.

The opening of Meadowfield and District Social Club, 2 June 1956. The show-piece club was opened by Mr Sid Lovers and cost around £41,000; it had 1,200 members when it opened. The club had been designed by one of its members, Mr Fred Hedley of Farnley Mount, Neville's Cross, who was also a surveyor to Brandon Urban District Council.

The Kings' College Folk Dance Team performing the Abbots Bromley Horn Dance at Brancepeth Church, 23 June 1956. The Durham Division English Folk Dance and Song Society held the Country Folk Dance Festival at Brancepeth Castle. The 300-year-old dance illustrated is performed annually at Abbots Bromley Church, Staffordshire.

Jacqueline Short and Charmian Duthie prepare posies for visitors to a garden party, which was held by the Durham Division of the Conservative & Unionist Association, in the grounds of Laxey Cottage, Shincliffe Village, 14 July 1956.

The Gaviole organ at Gilesgate Welfare Flower and Vegetable Show, 6 August 1956. One of the events was a 'most original dress' competition. The winner was June Thornton as 'Thing', a silver monster made up of squares boxes. Names in the group are: June Ivison, Sheila Blackmoor, John Naylor, Evelyn Gibson, George Savage, Keith James, Harry Thompson, Colin Shepherd, Rosemary Banham and Dorretta Savage. The Mayoress, Mrs E. Thurlow, mother of the mayor, opened the show.

The Leek Club Show of the General Gordon public house, Claypath, September 1956. It was said to be one of the oldest clubs in the city, having started out in 1926 as an onion club. Names: Tony Wills, George Walters, W. Shiell or Shields, A. Caulfield, D. Gibson, J. Sudder, F. Flynn, J. McManus, W. Turnbull, and landlord, D.R. Todd.

University Policeman, Mr A. Young with Miss Joy McKean, a North Island New Zealander, Palace Green, 25 September 1956. During the last 14 months her journey had read like a gazetteer-she had travelled 34,000 miles alone on her small 150cc two-stroke motorcycle. A farmer's daughter who had served as a nurse in Scotland during World War Two, she had left her home in Te Puke in July and travelled across Australia, India, East Africa, Cape Town and then through North Africa to Europe.

The first flower and vegetable show, of the drivers and HQ. saff of Durham Ambulance Service, Framwellgate Moor, September 1956. Stretchers were used as show benches. The judges were W. Bromley and J. Wilson of Brandon Colliery.

Durham City AFC, September 1956. Winner of the Durham Benevolent Bowl, it had defeated Crook Town at Spennymoor 4-2, before a crowd of 2,600. Back row, left to right: B. Nainby, G. Newton, M. Lax, G. Thompson, R. Ayre and E. Wilson. Front row, left to right: A. Smith, P. Nainby, N. Walton, F. Marshall and K. Williams.

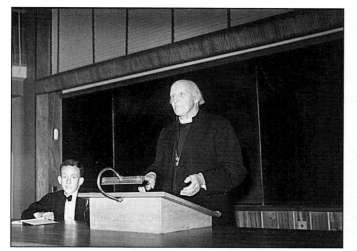

Durham City AFC, September 1956. Winner of the Durham Benevolent Bowl, it had defeated Crook Town at Spennymoor 4-2, before a crowd of 2,600. Back row, left to right: B. Nainby, G. Newton, M. Lax, G. Thompson, R. Ayre and E. Wilson. Front row, left to right: A. Smith, P. Nainby, N. Walton, F. Marshall and K. Williams. The Dean of Canterbury, Dr Hewlett Johnson, was giving a lecture on China when at eight minutes to nine, student pall-bearers entered the Appleby Lecture Theatre with an imitation coffin, draped in black, with the Hungarian flag overlaid, 13 November 1956. They laid it in front of the guest speaker and paid tribute to the Hungarian people whose revolution against their Soviet overlords was being crushed. This was part of a demonstration that students made, when the 'Red Dean' came to speak to Durham Colleges' UNSA & Social Society. Students also stole the Dean's hat and scarf and announced that it would be raffled for the Hungarian Relief Fund.

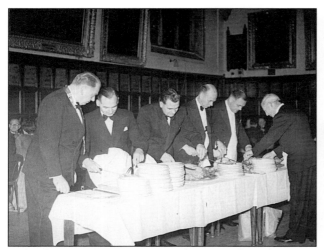

The Durham City & District Butchers'
annual dinner in the Town Hall, 21 November 1956. The
carvers with the joint of beef in the middle of the dance
floor were Councillor N. Williamson, Mr P. Newton,
Councillor R. Appleby, Mr C.W. Sample, Mr C. Guy and
Mr G. Lamb. After the meal the party danced to the music
of Norman Richardson's dance band.

Iris Dobson at her father's
(Ernie) pigeon loft, Broomside
Lane, Belmont, c.1956.

Framwellgate Moor's over 60s Christmas party, December 1956. It was held in the village school dining hall, 140 members were
entertained to tea and a concert.

1957

Mrs Mary Cairns, originally from Gilesgate, aged 71, surveying the dampness in her home, 52 New Elvet, January 1957. She was appealing, out of desperation, to be re-housed.

Student 'Rag', showing the 'Hatfield Flyer', travelling down Silver Street, 9 February 1957. The theme this year was 'Transport through the ages', referring to the Suez Canal crisis.

A sign erected near Kepier 'haughs' warning people that the river was polluted, March 1957. Concern over the state of the river had been raised by university lecturer, Dr K.R. Ashby, zoologist, who had put forward a four-point plan of action for cleaning the Wear, against the proposed plan of spending £7 million on the Derwent Valley Reservoir. On the right are the targets belonging to Kepier Rifle Range.

The final of the Durham Hospital Cup (founded 1910) at Ferens Park, Good Friday, April 1957. The carpet factory team was, back row, left to right: Eric Nicholson, Frank Smithson, Bobby Bell, Jimmy Crampton, Tommy Little and Kenny Reed. Front row: Danny Hardy, Ray McIllwrath, Charlie McArdle and Alan Davis. Other names in the group are: Albert Hughes (with towel), George Walters (holding his daughter), Harry Bond (centre rear) and back right, Reggie Scott, Steve O'Donnell, Jimmy West

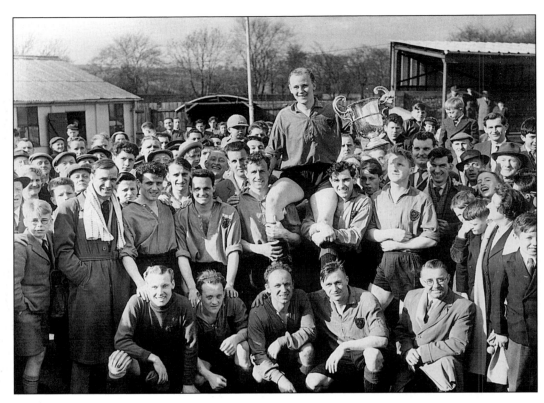

and Sid Welsbey. Mackay's carpet factory defeated Ushaw Moor 5-1 (four goals in the last 15 minutes). This was the first time Mackay's had won the trophy. The game was watched by 900 spectators.

T.D. Gargett, W.R. Armes and W.D. Stokes who represented Durham City Rovers (cycling club), in a 70-mile circular tour road race, which the club organised, starting from Witton Gilbert, May 1957.

A presentation of a long-service medal to housewife, Mrs Edna Warner of Merryoaks after 12 years service with the Royal Observer Corps, as Chief Woman Observer, May 1957. Capt.W.R. Wilkinson came from York to make the presentation. She joined the Corps in 1943 and apart from the two years when the entire Corps was disbanded, she had been a member of the Durham Group operations room.

Bluecoat School football team who played against Gilesgate Moor Council school (the 'Tin School') in the Minto Cup match, 17 May 1957. Gilesgate Moor, the holders, were defeated 4 goals to 3, the winning goal being scored by John Armstrong. Left to right: John Bates, Douglas Hutchinson, John Armstrong, Eddie Jenkins, Gerald Payne, Billy Stokoe, Tommy Stokoe, John O'Brien, Robert Cummings and Matty Beadall.

Brigadier J.M. Hanmer receives a group of medals formerly belonging to Pte. Michael Heaviside, VC, DLI, July 1957. Norman Heaviside, a grandson, presented the medals to the regiment for the regimental museum at Brancepeth Castle. He himself was a Dunkirk veteran and a miner, who had been connected with the DLI for 27 years. The medals were: The Victoria Cross, Queen's and King's South Africa Medals, The Mons Star, the General Service Medal, the Victory Medal and the Coronation Medal.

Mrs Elizabeth Cooper, aged 70, who before her second marriage, was the wife of Pte. Michael Heaviside, VC, July 1957. She is photographed looking up towards the three VCs that were displayed in the regimental museum. Her husband's medals were shortly to join them.

The Mayor and Mayoress, Alderman W.A.H. Shepherd and his daughter Edna, having fun with darts at the opening of the Gilesgate Welfare and Community Association's 12th annual flower show and gala, 5 August 1957.

Mr John Smith, left, manager of the ice-rink is photographed with Denis Smith, standing, a member of Cornsay Angling Club, seated are: John Ryans and Thomas Brown, of Ushaw Moor, 5 August 1957. Denis holds a 5lb sea trout which was caught near the rink. They had started fishing at around 4am, Millburngate Nursery is seen, top right.

Prize-winners at Gilesgate Allotments Association's annual show, August 1957. Left to right: unknown, unknown, George Coatham, Bill Irving, Reg Gleason, Jim Walton, Tony Wills, Ralph Gleason, Bob Elliott, unknown, Len Mitchinson, Bill Mason, Billy Green, George Mason, Tom Elliott, unknown, unknown.

Coal-miner. Corporal John Robert Bell, a married man with three children living at Brandon Colliery was picked to represent the 8th Battalion DLI at the Territorial Army Jubilee Celebrations that were being held the following year, October 1957. He is photographed at Brandon Pit House Colliery, telling his fellow miners the news of his selection.

Teddy Boy to chef, Peter Scott (second left), October 1957. He was the first person to complete his apprenticeship in the north under a new scheme, after five years intensive training in High Grade Cooking; he spent the last year training at the Three Tuns Hotel, New Elvet.

A golden wedding celebration at Vane Tempest Hall for Mr and Mrs F. Askew and Mr and Mrs Peace, arranged by St Giles's Mothers' Union and Young Wives' Club, November 1957.

Remembrance Day, Framwellgate Moor and District Branch of the British Legion pause at Pity Me war memorial, where Mr A. Field had placed a wreath, 11 November 1957.

Percy Cooper of Mowbray Street seen with colleagues on his last day at work as Station Inspector at Durham Railway Station, 13 November 1957. He was presented with a certificate from British Railways North-Eastern Area in recognition of his 43 years' service.

Mr James Ridley Brown, right, was the third member of his family to become a Freeman of Durham, 18 November 1957. His father, Charles Brown, is on the left, and his grandfather, William Ridley Brown, seated, had been a Freeman since 1908.

Durham's match against Tranmere Rovers, the second stage of the FA Cup-tie at Ferens Park, Football Stadium, 7 December 1957. Durham's team was S. Briggs, B. Nainby, G. Newton, R. Ayre, G.G. Thompson, E. Wilson, B. Armstrong, N. Walton, K. Bowron, J. Stevenson and Raine. Tranmere's team was Payne, Bell, Moore, Farrell, Millington, Charlton, McDevitt, Williams, Dodds, Crossan and Eglington.

Spectators at Durham Football Stadium for the match against Tranmere Rovers, 7 December 1957. The record attendance was 7,000, even the Bishop of Jarrow the Right Revd J.A. Ramsbotham, turned up with his daughter; Unfortunately Durham lost to Tranmere 3-0. The last time the two clubs had met was 7 January 1928 at Birkenhead, when Tranmere defeated Durham 11-1.

Durham City football club's trainer at Ferens Park, the man with the 'Magic' sponge, Herbie Ingram, December 1957. For many years he was janitor at Durham Town Hall and Mayor's Swordbearer.

The Mayor, Councillor W.A.H. Shepherd, at the lighting of Durham Round Table's Christmas tree in the Market Place, December 1957. Children had brought gifts to the tree to be given out later to children who were less fortunate.

The Mayor, Alderman W.A.H. Shepherd, was the guest of the members of the Tankard Club at the Shakespeare Tavern, Saddler Street, on the occasion of their Christmas dinner, December 1957.

1958

A presentation of a gold watch at Baxter Wood No.2 signal box to Mr J. Dent of Durham, to mark his 49 years service with British Railways, 7 January 1958. Mr A. Bowes, Station-master at Brandon Colliery, left, attended the presentation, which was made by Mr E. McClelland of Darlington.

The Farm Stores, a well known pork butchers' shop, photographed on the day of the opening of its first shop in Durham City, on Framwellgate Bridge, January 1958. They had branches in all the principal towns and cities of Yorkshire and Durham.

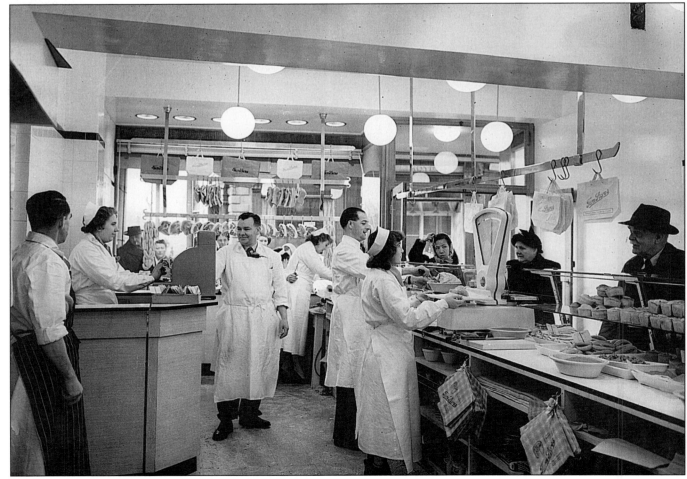

A presentation of a chiming clock to Earl Carlson by the Mayor, Alderman Shepherd, January 1958. This was a gift from his team-mates and the ice-rink management to mark his 500 goals for the Wasps ice-hockey team. Third from the right, standing, is George Lye of Fillingham's photography shop.

Student 'Rag', 8 February 1958. A publicity stunt by students in the icy river near Millburngate. The terraced buildings are Lambton Walk, demolished for the Millburngate Shopping Centre.

A wagon loaned by Simpson's, Roofing Contractors of Gilesgate, passing over Framwellgate Bridge carrying students during the 'Rag' procession, 8 February 1958.

Students parading down Castle Chare past The Royal Hotel during their 'Rag' procession, 8 February 1958. They were hoping to raise £2,500 for Dr Barnardo's Home. By the end of the evening a count revealed almost £3,500.

'Tisker', queen of the Horse-Hole, Millburngate, February 1958. The official rat-catcher, of the Gas Company, she is photographed with her owner, Charlie Clark, foreman, who had worked for the company for 34 years. Charlie had rescued the cat from the river two years earlier.

Dennis Cunningham, butcher from Bearpark, in his father's shop, March 1958. He was also an amateur comedian and had performed at numerous Women's Institute groups and operatic societies. His customers are, left to right: Mrs Urwin, Jimmy Grady and Mrs Todd. Dennis' grandfather had started the business at Bearpark in 1895.

Councillor Mrs E. Robson, photographed with Mr George Brown, Clerk to the Parish Council, opening the King George V Memorial Playing Field at Framwellgate Moor, 22 March 1958. It was once a disused pit-heap and was purchased from the Durham County Council for £120. The making of the playing field cost £8,300 of which £2,150 was from the King George V Memorial Foundation.

The 'Peter Pan' of Durham Baths, Robert Mackay (69) of Craghead, who made a weekly visit to the baths where he taught youngsters to swim and dive, April 1958.

Victorious Belmont (3-2) after the Durham Minor Cup Final, against Witton Park, 19 April 1958. Holding the cup is Captain Fred Crago. Names of the Belmont team are: S. Sweat, B. Nichols, A. Bertram, J. Hill, E. Wright, J. Walton, A. Piper, K. Greenwood, G. Marley, F. Crago and D. Clough.

MAYNARDS LTD

WILL'S's
CAPSTAN

SOLD HERE
Wall's
ICE CREAM

POLO

Wall's
ICE CREAM
FRUIT
ICES

Best of all—
Smoke
WOODBINES

the GREAT little cigarette

WILD
WOODBINE
ARETTES

Wall's
ICE CREAM
SOLD HERE

WOODBINES

PLAYER'S
NAVY C

CIGARETT
MEDIUM

Maynard's sweet
shop, Saddler Street,
April 1958. The
photograph was
taken to highlight
the growing concern
over shop front
advertisements.

To commemorate the centenary of St Hild's College (1858-1958) Sir Hector Hetherington planted a tree in the grounds, assisted by the Archbishop of York, Dr A.M. Ramsey, May 1958.

The three oldest past students of St Hild's College attending the reunion at the colleges centenary celebrations, May 1958. Left to right: Mrs M.S. Fletcher, aged 95, Mrs F. Bennett, aged 94, and Mrs M. Martin, aged 87. It was the custom at the college to present a pot of flowers to the three oldest students attending.

Shoppers leaving Claypath walking towards the Market Place, 2 May 1958. The buildings seen on the left are Fleming & Neil, Ironmongers, The Wheatsheaf public house unknown, and the Co-operative Store. The Claypath underpass now occupies that site.

NO WAITING 8 - 8 AM PM

One of the white peacocks in the courtyard of Brancepeth Castle, which was then the headquarters of the Durham Light Infantry, May 1958. The peacocks were under the personal charge of a NCO, who was especially detailed to look after them.

Durham City Senior School, Whinney Hill, Elvet, June 1958, showing the girls' entrance. The school was opened by Brig. Gen. Sir Conyers Surtees KT, 15 September 1932. The architect was the city engineer, Mr J.W. Green. The tall chimney belongs to the prison boiler house.

The first visit of Her Royal Highness Princess Alexandra to the regiment (DLI), since being appointed by the Queen as Colonel-in Chief, 17 May 1958. She was taking part in the Regiment's bi-centenary celebrations. Durham Market Place was crowded to watch her take the salute at the march past. The entire regiment, including 220 of the old comrades and also representatives from the army cadet forces of the county, took part.

The Mayor, Councillor J.A. Naylor, centre, welcoming overseas bishops who were attending the Lambeth Conference, 11 June 1958. While in England they visited the Diocese of Durham, accompanied by the Bishop of Durham. Left to right: the Rt. Revd Ezra Douglas Martinson, Assistant Bishop of Accra; the Rt. Revd M.H. Harland, Bishop of Durham; the Rt.Revd Allen Howard Johnson, Bishop of Dunedin and the Rt. Revd Lucian Charles Usher-Wilson, Bishop of the Upper Nile.

The Roman Catholic Churches of Durham held their Garden Fete in the grounds of St Leonard's, RC School, June 1958. The Mayor, Councillor J.A. Naylor, tries his luck at the shooting gallery after he opened the fair. Behind the children is Councillor W. Edge.

The County Rally at Houghall, 21 June 1958. Lads of the County Federation of Young Farmers' Club had the 'Tossing the Sheaf' competition to themselves, until Durham farmers' daughter, Joy Kingston, came along to stake a claim for the lassies. Over 3,000 visitors attended the 17th annual rally.

Assistant Commissioner of Durham County Scout Association, Dr J.A. Chalmers (affectionately known as 'Skip'), at the opening of the new headquarters for the 1st Brandon Scout Troop, 16 July 1958. The building was formerly the premises of Brandon Social Club.

Alderman and Mrs Wilf Edge ready to take their grandson, Kenneth, on his first pilgrimage to Lourdes, 31 July 1958. The Bishop of Hexham and Newcastle, the Rt. Revd James Cunningham, greeted 100 pilgrims from the Durham area when they boarded the train at Durham Station to join the pilgrims already on the train.

Mr John Roach of Framwellgate Moor, a watch repairer, August 1958. He had been a blacksmith at Bearpark Colliery, until an injury forced him to seek light employment. The photograph shows him with some of the many paintings he exhibited in the studio of John Craggs, Saddler Street. He had exhibited at the Laing and Shipley Art Galleries in Newcastle and Gateshead, respectively, also in London.

The 'Deputies' Kist' at the Travellers' Rest public house, Framwellgate Moor, August 1958. Mr Herbert Hoggett had decorated his bar with a selection of his 22 miners' lamps and various other pit memorabilia.

The Mayoress, Mrs G.M. Oates, judging the fancy dress parade at Vane Tempest Hall, 4 August 1958. She was accompanied by the Mayor, Councillor J.A. Naylor, the Deputy Mayor, Alderman Shepherd, and his daughter, Edna the Deputy Mayoress.

Methodists from Sherburn Village organised a field day in the 'Welfare Field' in aid of the fund for the new chapel, 23 August 1958. About £60 was raised.

The *Durham County Advertiser* caption, September 1958, read: 'Perhaps I don't come under these parking laws? Anyway my boss said he would be a jiffy', while he 'signed on' at Durham Employment Exchange, Saddler Street.

The newly-appointed Master of Sherburn Hospital, Canon Jack Norwood, is photographed in the hospital grounds with some of the brethren, September 1958. A graduate of University College, London, he was ordained in 1932. After holding curacies at Dalton-le-Dale and Brandon, he became vicar of St Aidan's, South Shields, and later (1946) vicar of St Giles's, Durham. He was also Rural Dean prior to his appointment to the hospital.

Children from Neville's Cross School and students from Durham Commercial College who presented the carol play, 'Nowell', at St Cuthbert's Church, North Road, 19 December 1958. The play was an adaptation from the Coventry and Wakefield Mystery plays. Some of the names are: P. Crawford, M. Rose. J. Mole, R. Davidson, G. Lowe, J. Stoker, M. Reed, J. Ward, E. Alderson, D. Lauderdale, B. Moore, R. Swinburn, S. Eccleston, C. Merick, J. Pearson, L. Daglish, D. Smith, K. Pearson, J. Smith, R. Ellis and W. Duffy.

1959

Young soldiers pose for a photograph at Durham Railway Station before their journey to Cyprus to join the 1st Battalion Durham Light Infantry, February 1959.

Peter Tones, aged 16, a Johnston schoolboy photographed on his parents' smallholding, near Bearpark, March 1959. His runabout, named Wells Fargo, was used to tour the farm.

A barn fire at Old Durham Farm, May 1959. About 20 tons of hay and straw were destroyed, as well as 600 fencing posts valued at about £75. The wall on the left belongs to the 17th-century walled garden of the former manor house.

Durham School, summer fete, May 1959. The ingenious contraption was made by boys from the school; a hit in the right place sent a bucket of sawdust down on the victim.

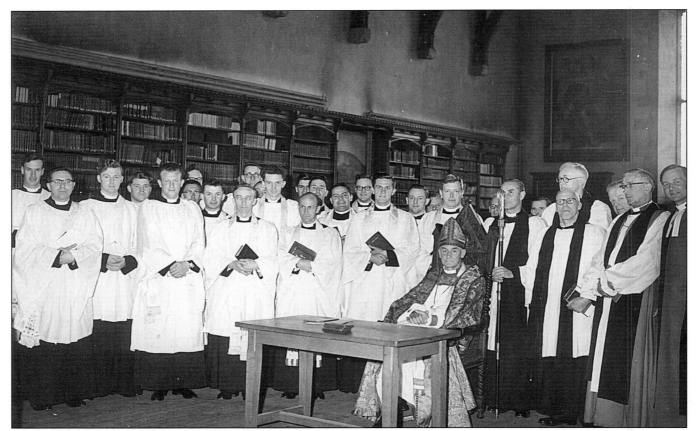

A presentation of 'letters of order' by the Bishop of Durham the Rt. Revd M.H. Harland, to candidates who were ordained at the cathedral, 24 May 1959. They were photographed in the Monks' Dormitory. The candidates were, Deacons: A. Gales, A. Hawell, R.M.C. Jeffery, W.W. Lucas, A.W.D. Ritson, J.A. Turner and M.R. Welsh. Priests: S.R. Burrows, C. Charlton, L. Constantine, J.F. Forbes, H.H.S.L. Hall, E.G. Leshnick, D. O'Connor, M.T. Peach, P.D. Stubley, N.L.A. Tidwell, K.I. Woodhouse and E. Zachau.

A folk-dance rally at Brancepeth Castle, organised by the Durham County Federation of Women's Institutes, 13 June 1959. For nearly five hours 800 women danced intricate steps.

Elvet Bridge and Brown's Boat House on Regatta Day, 20 June 1959. A record number of 200 entries took part this year.

A celebration gathering at the laying of the foundation stone for Durham City Baptist Church, Sunderland Road, 20 June 1959. The Revd J.R. Barrett of Leeds, Area Superintendent conducted the ceremony. The four central figures are, left to right: Mr and Mrs J. Cheek, Dan Nicholls and the Revd Roy W. Williams. The church was founded in October 1950 with a membership of six.

Pensioners from Sunderland Road Estate, prior to their journey to the seaside, August 1959. Bill Molyneux provided the music on the way with his squeeze-box.

J. & G. Archibalds' stand at the County Show, August 1959. Councillor Gordon McIntyre, Managing Director, is on the far right.

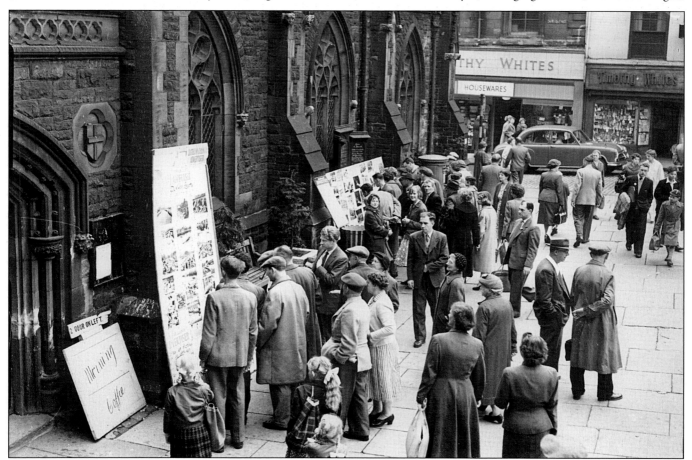

The *Durham County Advertiser* display in Durham Market Place during the newspaper strike, which lasted about seven weeks, August 1959.

Riders of the newly-formed Durham City Motor Cycle Club, gathered outside the city for the start of their first road trial, 13 September 1959. Mr Bob Fletcher of the Volunteer Arms, Gilesgate, is holding the silver cup which he donated for the occasion. He started the 125-mile race. Ian Carr of Spennymoor, and his navigator, John Robinson of Sacriston, won the Fletcher Cup.

A collection of trade union badges belonging to Mr Frank Illingworth of Lowes Barn Bank, Secretary of the North-East Federation of Trades Councils, October 1959. He had collected over 150 badges from all parts of the world. One of his oldest, dated 1870, belonged to the Amalgamated Association of Railway Servants.

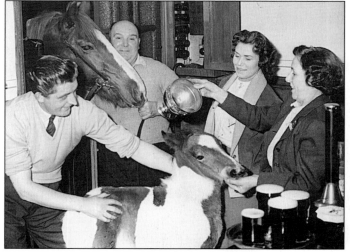

Nine-year-old Kitty and her piebald foal, Nancy, at the christening in the Brewers' Arms, Gilesgate, 25 November 1959. Only a fortnight before a vet confirmed that Kitty was expecting. During the day she dragged a scrap-metal cart up and down the streets of the city. The news was a big surprise to her owner, Mr Charlie Newton junior. The foal was named Nancy after the landlady, Mrs Dowse, pictured with her arms around the foal's neck. After the birth, Kitty had a four-month holiday before returning to work.

A cat-rescue from the River Wear at Millburngate, 26 November 1959. After a one-hour operation Sub Officer Reg James and Fire Officer Anthony Temple brought the cat to safety. Waiting at the riverside was Miss Gwen Wilkinson (see p.109), Secretary of the local branch of the RSPCA, who put 'Ginger' into a shopping bag and took it home for a meal and dry-out.

Children cross the busy road outside Gilesgate Council School, Sunderland Road, December 1959. The school was demolished several years ago and council bungalows were built on the site. The terraced buildings on the right are the rear of Young Street.

Sherburn Hill Colliery Band honoured Jackie Kell, with the presentation of a silver tankard following his 67 years service with the Band, December 1959. He had joined the band at the age of 13, in 1892, and had never missed playing at the 'Big Meeting'. He is photographed with his grandson, Graham.

1960

Durham Town Hall was transformed into a variety theatre where star turns from the city and district, gave a show, January 1960. One such turn was The Sapphire Harmony Group, left to right: Billy Cole, Frank Gill, George Kell and Kenny Morgan.

The Diamonds, c.1960. Left to right: Arthur Crampton, Peter Wendle, Wilf Carr, Colin Salisbury and Alan Clark. The group was the resident band at the Wearmouth Hotel, Claypath, and also played at other clubs and public houses around the Durham area.

Norman Richardson, travel agent, 107 Claypath, January 1960. He opened Durham's first travel bureau in 1947, also in Claypath. An ex-Johnston schoolboy, he joined the RAF, shortly after the outbreak of World War Two as a pilot. He undertook 52 operational flights, most of them with the famed Pathfinders. On 22 May 1963 he was elected Mayor of Durham.

Durham's bus depot's £80,000 extension, Waddington Street, January 1960. The work was carried out by a local firm, R.E. Coleman, Western Hill. Further service pits were installed containing heating appliances and fluorescent lighting.

Empire Buildings, Sherburn Road, February 1960. The private road in front of the shops was in such a bad state that the large pool was almost 10in deep.

Mrs Molly Caulfield, licensee of the Criterion Hotel (now the site of the Coach and Eight) and her husband, Alf, photographed with their dog, 21-year-old Prince, and his new friend, Tess the Alsatian, February 1960. Mrs Caulfield had rescued the latter from being destroyed.

A raft-race at the student 'Rag', February 1960. The first prize was a barrel of beer, which was won by the Grey College Crew. Money raised that year was given to the World Refugee Fund (£4,690 13s 11d).

A General Post Office supply wagon which crashed into a City Council store-yard in Providence Row, when making a delivery to the Durham Telephone Exchange, 29 February 1960.

An early morning surprise in Crossgate, after part of St Margaret's Churchyard wall collapsed during the night, March 1960. Council workmen are seen making the site safe.

Road works in the Market Place, 16 March 1960. Workmen were laying ducts for cables which were to lead to the new sub-station at the rear of Woolworths. The second, and last, Police Box can be seen. This was removed on 18 November 1975.

The new crematorium, South Road, March 1960. Inspiration for the whole of the design was drawn from Durham's buildings. The architect was Mr J.B. Chaplin. He chose the octagonal shape, as it was a feature of the city's ancient architecture, for example the Castle Keep and the Monks' Kitchen. The stone columns were in the rounded Norman style and made of local Dunhouse stone. The cost was about £60,000. The chapel was dedicated 3 August 1960, by the Rt Revd Dr Maurice Harland, Bishop of Durham.

Mr A. Caulfield, husband of the licensee of the Criterion, opening one of the many bottles of wine which were discovered in a room in the cellar that had not been used for years, March 1960. This was full of old brewery equipment and records which had belonged to T. & H.C. Colpitts, who were the early owners.

Mr Eddy Winter, foreman at Long Myers Farm, Sherburn, weighing piglets at three to eight weeks old, to check growth rate and the sows' mothering ability, March 1960. The farm was occupied by Gordon Gilson and was part of the Sherburn Hospital Estate.

Some of the 15 members of the Durham Marquetry Club who met at Alington House, North Bailey, March 1960. A fascinating display of their work was on display in the Town Hall.

Miss Lydia Hinds (headmistress) with her last pupils at the closing of Littletown School, 8 April 1960. The building had opened in January 1875. A new modern school at Sherburn Village was to take its place.

Crates of oranges were turned into 'orange squash' when part of this load scattered its contents over the road in Sutton Street, near the County Hospital, April 1960.

An Easter egg competition that was held at the Sun Inn, 34 Hallgarth Street, April 1960. Arranged by the Tankard Club, it consisted of 72 painted and dyed eggs.

Durham Amateur Operatic Society's cast of The Quaker Girl, a musical comedy set in Edwardian times. It was produced by Mr Ray Naylor, and was presented at the Assembly Rooms, North Bailey, April 1960. The photograph of the cast was taken in Dun Cow Lane. Names of some of them are: Derek Turner, Edith Carvill, Frank Rodwell, George Hetherington, Bob Christie, Elizabeth Duffy, Ann Curry, Jim Carvill, Margaret Bailes, Marjorie Sarsfield, Oliver Heron, Horace Myers, Margaret Todd, Meg Stenson, Stanley Crabtree, Helen Sowerby, Jeffrey Young, Ted Darkers, Jimmy Mein and Wilf Anderson.

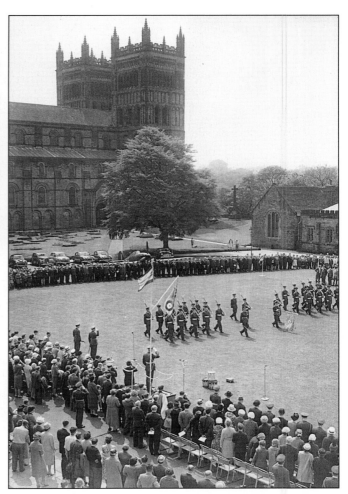

A helicopter of the Queen's Flight arriving at Durham Technical College for a test take-off, 17 May 1960. This was in preparation for the Duke of Edinburgh's visit to the college on 24 June. The Duke was to arrive by train at 10am and leave by helicopter for Darlington at 12.15pm.

Right and below: The consecration of the 607 Squadron Standard, 22 May 1960. Two former World War One Royal Flying Corps pilots, Durham's 'flying bishop', Dr Maurice Harland, and the Mayor, Sir James Duff, were among the squadron of the Royal Auxiliary Air Force at the Palace Green ceremony. Dean J.H.S. Wild consecrated the standard before it was laid up in the cathedral. It was to hang over the squadron's war memorial in the South Transept.

The Gulbenkian Museum for Art and Archaeology of the Far East (commonly called the Oriental Museum), 28 May 1960. The Earl of Scarborough, Chancellor of Durham University, formally opened it. Part of the School of Oriental Studies it cost £60,000 to build. It was designed by the firm of Middleton Fletcher of Middlesbrough.

Dr M.H. Harland, the Bishop of Durham, accepted Yatty Johnston's advice when he was challenged by Jim English to a game of dominoes, at Craghead British Legion Club, June 1960. This was the first time the Bishop had played, so he did well (thanks to Yatty) to be beaten by two spots. Dr Harland was visiting the club during his tour of Craghead.

A visit to Durham Technical College by the Duke of Edinburgh, 29 June 1960. He had come to visit a cross-section of youthful achievement, in connection with his Award Scheme. He spent more than an hour inspecting 36 youth organisations from the County which were taking part. He also presented over 100 awards. The Duke is seen at the Police Cadet display.

St Godric's RC School, Castle Chare, Durham, Sister Gabriel (left), and Sister Ursula (right), July 1960. After 63 years of teaching by the Sisters of Mercy at Durham these two nuns were the last of them, and were returning to St Ann's Convent in Newcastle.

An embarrassed driver explains his mishap to a passing policeman outside the Shakespeare Inn, Saddler Street, July 1960. The wagonload of flour had broken the trap door to the cellar when driving over it.

Miss Emma Crampton aged 74 and her niece Mrs Ivy Radstock of Oswald Court photographed in their beautiful garden, August 1960. They were winners for the fifth time in the 'flowers-only class' of the council garden competition. The gardens are still well cared for in this area.

The laying of new road surfaces in Saddler Street, 1 October 1960. The photograph was taken at 11pm, and shows council workmen who were busy all through the night removing the old granite sets. It was a race against time for the 18 employees of Durham City Council to finish before the morning traffic.

The 'tea man', Fossy Hall of Gilesgate, preparing the tea for his work-mates outside the employment office, Saddler Street, 1 October 1960. Many will remember him collecting scrap-wood to make into fire-wood.

The travelling busker at the top of the Magdalene Steps, Saddler Street, 21 September 1960. Tom Webb was an ex-artilleryman who had suffered a leg injury in World War One. Originally from Nottingham, he was a frequent visitor in the streets of Durham with his accordion and trumpet.

Mr Fred Docherty, gentlemen's outfitter, North Road, boards up his window for the second time that year due to a spot of trouble on Saturday nights, 16 October 1960.

A Cairn terrier waiting for his master outside the north door of the cathedral, October 1960. It was used in the *Durham County Advertiser* with the caption: 'Dear me, I hope he remembers I'm still here'.

Soldiers from the Durham Light Infantry view the silver cross and candlesticks, after the Rt Revd M.H. Harland, Bishop of Durham, had dedicated them in the regimental chapel at Durham Cathedral, 16 October 1960. The Chapel was dedicated to the Durham Light Infantry in 1924.

Prize-winners at speech day, Bluecoat School, Claypath, 21 October 1960.

Miss Gwen Wilkinson of South Street, Durham City, October 1960. The daughter and granddaughter of Northern clergymen, she was born at Hebburn-on-Tyne and came to Durham about 1940, where she lived with an aunt at Grafton House, South Street. She was Honorary Secretary of the Durham Branch of the RSPCA and was involved with many voluntary bodies, as well as with the Royal Observer Corps.

Gilesgate Welfare Association's, Autumn Fair, showing a display by the Model Engineering Society, November 1960.

Competitors who took part in the Central Division YOC Annual Swimming Gala, when boys of the 5th Durham Scouts won both the Senior and Junior YOC trophy, November 1960.

Mr Stanley Rankin of Cedar Drive, Farewell Hall, a keen bird-fancier, in his aviary. This contained more than 100 foreign birds from 28 countries, November 1960. In his first three shows he won over 20 prizes.

One of two old cannons outside the Territorial headquarters, Old Elvet, October-November 1960. They were made in Scotland during the Napoleonic Wars by the Carron Iron Company, Falkirk. These examples were salvaged from a shipwreck near Tynemouth Lifeboat Station. They were brought from there to Durham in the 1950s, by the CO of the Territorial and Army Volunteer Reserve. On the left is Lt Col C.F. Hutchinson DSO, OBE, DL, secretary of the Durham Territorial and Auxiliary Forces.

Passengers wait at the bus-stand outside the National Provincial Bank, Market Place for the most expensive bus-ride in the city, December 1960. The Durham District Service's journey Market Place to Whitesmocks, had risen from 3½d to 4½d for the second time in two years. At the time the fare was almost the same as that of taking a taxi.

OTHER BOOKS AVAILABLE FROM BREEDON BOOKS

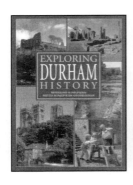